Skyline
2017

Cyberworld Publishing

www.CyberworldPublishing.com

Cyberworld Publishing
Toronto, NSW, 2283
Australia

Skyline 2017

*An Anthology of
Prose and Poetry by
Central Virginia Writers*

Olivia Stowe, ed.

Skyline 2017 is dedicated to the memory of

Sharon Leiter

August 1942 – January 2016

Former President, Charlottesville Writers Chapter, VWC

Poet and Fiction Writer

Instructor in Literature and Creative Writing, University of Virginia

Skyline 2015 Featured Poet

Table of Contents

Prose Nonfiction

On Writing/Publishing

Introduction

Skyline 2017, the fourth in a series of annual publisher's anthologies produced by Cyberworld Publishing, showcases the prose and poetry talents of Central Virginia writers. The title of the anthology is taken from the Skyline Drive, the parkway skipping along the top of the Blue Ridge Mountains in Virginia and providing centering for the region in which the authors showcased here are living and writing. Thus far the editions have followed the seasons in cover image, with this being the summer edition.

Other than the *Skyline* Summer contest works, there is no overarching theme for the short stories, poems, and essays in this anthology, so each can be discovered and appreciated on its own context and merits. Over half of the works found here won or placed in various Virginia regional and statewide writing contests between September 2015 and September 2016. The foundation for the juried contest selections included consists of the 2016 writing contest of the Blue Ridge Writers Chapter of the Virginia Writers Club (VWC), a 2016 *Skyline* Summer writing contest, and the 2016 poetry awards of the Poetry Society of Virginia. Also included in the anthology are representative works by the *Skyline* Summer contest judges and *Skyline* volume editor, established writers all. Additional works include pieces from the portfolios of the contest selectees and special contributor works by established writers in the Central Virginia region.

The anthology is made up of fifty-two works by twenty-nine authors, presented in four sections: fiction (twelve short stories), poetry (twenty-three poems), nonfiction (twelve essays), and, since this is a writer's anthology, a section on writing and publishing (five essays). Eclectic is the hallmark word for this collection. Half of the authors here are represented by more than one work and in varied media to showcase their writing skills.

A notable additional section to this anthology is the "About the Authors" section, which provides fascinating, I think, literary background notes on the authors represented in this collection as well as the judges for the 2016 *Skyline*

Summer writing contest. Sarah Collins Honenberger, former Virginia Writers Club Charlottesville Writers Chapter president and author of four published novels, judged the fiction section. Lori Dixon, establish judge for VWC and Poetry Society of Virginia contests, judged the poetry section. Becky Mushko, former VWC board member and Appalachian novelist and essayist, judged the nonfiction section.

As with the three earlier annual *Skyline* editions, it has been a delight to work with and discover the many varied themes and high quality of writing of these Central Virginia writers. I hope you will find these works as fresh and as entertaining and thought provoking as I have. These indeed are exceptional writers who deserve to have their works highlighted and represented in the marketplace.

Olivia Stowe
Volume Editor
Skyline 2017

PROSE FICTION

Baby-Faced Wolf

Jody Hobbs Hesler

It's so hot every day you can see heat wiggling off the pavement in blurry waves. The pollen covers everything in layers and layers of yellow dust, and it doesn't rain. You'd think we'd all walk around in a stupor and all we'd talk about would be Caitlin. But what can we say? None of us knows what happened. They found one shoe by the river, another somewhere in town. It doesn't make sense. Anyway, we're fourteen, fifteen, and we figure nothing bad in the world can ever happen to us, even if it did happen to Caitlin Ward.

Missy Simpkin's sister tells a scary story about this wild animal that roams the mountainside with the body of a wolf and the face of a baby. It's one of those stories you only believe at night, when you're walking home alone along one of the dirt roads. Any noise, any flicker in the moonlight, and you're sure that baby-faced wolf has found you. But in the daylight, it's just a scary story, a silly one, even. That's what we think about Caitlin Ward.

The fair comes into town like it always does, with fliers posted on phone poles all through town, flapping in the breezes, showing up wind-tattered and faded against the curbs and in the parking lot of the Shop and Go. That's all that ever happens in the summers, the fair coming and going. Then school starts again.

By the time the fair starts, Caitlin has been gone three weeks. There's a sign up at the bank where her daddy works, declaring the number of days: 9, 16, 22.

Just like any summer, we walk around town barefoot, zeroing in on the day's hangout. Sometimes it's the river, sometimes the newsstand that still sells candy for a dime, sometimes the Hamburger Hut where we get milkshakes.

You would think we wouldn't walk alone in a summer like this, but we do. Every odd now and then, when a pickup truck slows down alongside you, you think about Caitlin Ward. One shoe here, one shoe there. What ever happened between? Then you look up and see old Bernie Towson leering out at you from behind his steering wheel, letting out some creepy whistle from between his tongue and teeth like he always does. You flip him the bird, tell him to fuck off, and that's that.

Down at the fairgrounds, everything's the same, too. Groups of us hang out by the exhibit entrances, where the farm animals are driven in and out. Sometimes, from there, we can sneak in for free because it's way too expensive to pay every day. Otherwise, we just hang out, chewing gum and smoking cigarettes.

Once Eddie Barton brought some vodka from his parents' stash. By lunchtime we were all drunk and throwing up. Luckily, it was a hot day so all our parents thought we'd just been in the sun too long. Lily Penderson passed out, even, and got treated for dehydration. We thought the doctor might get wise to us, but he just gave her Gatorade after Gatorade. We all thought it was hilarious how heat exhaustion and total drunkenness looked about the same. Still, Eddie hasn't brought vodka since.

The exhibitors are the only people we see besides each other. There's this one guy who drives in behind a livestock truck full of cattle. He must be at least sixteen, because he drives a powder blue pickup, older than me. His sun-browned arm sticks out the window as he rolls past. Then he walks by, getting the fence opened and closed, and we can see him unloading all his prize-winning cows from where we're standing. The first day he unloads the cows, the next days he just comes through there to show them, I guess. But every day he wears a pair of ragged old overalls, no shirt underneath. Missy Simpkins laughs about how he probably doesn't have anything else on under there. It's something we wonder about every time we see him.

One day he winds up standing right in front of me. He dropped something when he got out to shut the gates. He leans over to pick it up, and I run smack into him. So there he is, looking me right in the face. His eyes match his truck. He's so tan he looks like a big piece of chocolate, and his black hair flops into his eyes. "Hi," he says, without a hint of shyness. So I say hi back, and a thrill runs up my spine.

The guy who made off with Caitlin Ward, he could've

been somebody like this, somebody who's only in town a short time, somebody nobody knows nor has a chance to question or doubt before he disappears and is gone forever. It makes my heart beat fast enough it feels clogged up. It's already hot, so I'm already sweating.

The next day he says hi, too, and the next day he motions for me to come in the gates with him. He introduces me to all his cows. His are dairy cows, which I think is funny, a gorgeous boy like him showing a bunch of prissy girl cows with curly eyelashes just so he can get a blue ribbon and his name in the paper. But it's sweet, too, so I act interested and listen to all their names, to all the work he does to get them show ready.

The air in the stalls smells of hay and manure and is thick with hayseed dust, swirling pollen, and loads of bugs aiming for the livestock. After he gives me a tour, we walk down the fairway. He shoots a few plastic ducks and wins me a blue teddy bear. Then he buys me a rainbow snow cone with change he dredges out of the bottom of those overall pockets. The sun is hot, the air thick enough to choke you.

Last of all, he walks me out back behind the Ferris wheel and into a shed full of supplies, like extra napkins for the funnel cakes and prizes yet to be won. Back there he leans his long body against mine and kisses me. My face is sticky from the snow cone, and my heart is really pounding now. He slides his dirt-caked hands up under my T-shirt and touches my breasts, the first boy who's ever done that. I don't know what would've happened if Mr. Proudhammer, the emcee of the livestock show, hadn't reached his hand inside the shed at just that moment and thrown open the door. "Miss Tanya!" he roars in surprise, seeing me, and before you can blink, that overalled boy is out of sight and gone for good.

I head for home, barefoot, lugging my little blue bear, my heart still thudding against my chest, my stomach fizzing like soda. Maybe some of it's shame because I don't even know the boy's name, but some of it's thrills.

Walking on through Main Street back toward the hill where my house is, I pass the Wards in the Shop and Go parking lot, all hollow-eyed and pale. Mrs. Ward walks slumped over with a silver cardigan wrapped around her shoulders, as if

19

she could be cold on such a day. When I see them all, Mr. and Mrs. Ward and their other two children, it's like their eyes glue onto me. It's like they can see that I've been holed up in a shed with a boy, letting him touch me, having his tongue in my mouth and his hand up my shirt, being so perfectly alive.

Their heads turn in continuous motion as I pass. I can see their thoughts on their faces. Why isn't that Caitlin? Why can't we be worried about a dark little shed on the edge of the fairground? A girl who might wind up pregnant? And I can see them running their eyes up and down my body, at the way my breasts filled out my T-shirt for the first time this summer, at the little rivers of sweat going down my face, soaking my shirt and the pieces of hair sticking out from my braid. I can see that they would take me just as I am, at any price, if I could be Caitlin. They would swoop down on me, wrap me in satin, clean my body from the inside out till I would shine like the sun. They would kiss every toe on my feet, if I would be Caitlin.

But I'm not thinking of Caitlin, not for long. I'm thinking of that boy's fingers along my bare ribs, the moist heat of his breath on my neck, and how maybe he'll be there again tomorrow.

Robert Frost, Where Are You?

Sarah Collins Honenberger

The wall wasn't the whole problem. Or the real problem. Even if you knew nothing about engineering or our neighbors, it was obvious the wall was the tip of an iceberg.

The summer the seawall failed I was fifteen, "a tall drink of water" my grandfather Gene used to announce, as if it were the endorsement of a hidden talent only a psychic could discern. Eugene Francis Taliaferro, the youngest son of an Italian immigrant, was not a short man himself, already stoop-shouldered when I knew him, the first Taliaferro to graduate college. Growing up Frankie, he fit in wherever he went. Half the neighbors thought he was Irish, which saved him many a bloody nose to hear his side of it. And the other half knew he was Italian because they knew his older brothers, Benito and Joseph, street toughs who plowed through jobs and girls without a plan in their heads except where they'd scarf the next beer.

The way PawPaw Gene told the story, the day he received his acceptance from the small Presbyterian college he packed his other shirt and his extra pair of navy pants along with his thrift-store copy of *Walden* in his canvas rucksack and left a note.

"Off to study economics; will write once I'm settled."

No endearment for his mother with the bad hip, no details for his father, the traveling salesman who lived in his car more than the family's rented row house near Philly's Washington Street market, no playful slug to the shoulder of either brother. When PawPaw left them all behind—Mom told me this, part warning, part family skeleton—he tossed the name Frankie too, forever after introducing himself as Gene, a name he felt conveyed an easy confidence, a visible complement to his purposeful stride, his expressive hands, and his endless supply of jokes. He wanted people to like him, and they did.

Somehow I knew, even at fifteen, that if my grandfather had been alive when the wall failed, things would have turned out differently.

* * * *

The first hint of trouble appeared in February—a melting snow, an ominous indentation several hundred feet from the house. The clapboard cottage where I'd lived my whole life with its oddly juxtaposed wings was a retreat for my father, Gene's namesake, who couldn't keep a job. I was never sure whether the drinking problem came before or after his paralyzing fear of failure, inspired by a father who was the first to tell you he had climbed Mount Everest. PawPaw was a storyteller and stories beget legends.

The ground must have started to sink weeks before Dad decided to investigate; its staying power and Mom's complaints earned the closer inspection. When he struck out across the splotches of leftover snow, I was hunched over my desk in fleece-lined jeans and a double pair of socks. Wedged under the eaves, my room was carved from attic, a cramped space darkened by the overhang, but with the best sunset view of the marsh. Except no one knew because no one else ever came up.

The original cottage was too small for a third child, a late and unexpected baby. Before I was schooled in Roman Catholic canons of conjugal sex, I fabricated an explanation of why me, why ten years after my brothers. It didn't take much imagination. Frank and Danny had worn Mom out. She had to recuperate after the onslaught of laundry and discipline and food production necessary to corral the tornado that dogged Frank and Danny like a new puppy.

Only since my own entanglement with girls did I realize Mom's exhaustion may have had more to do with Dad's drinking and problems at work. Sex, I was just discovering, could be celebration or despair, the last lunge of hand for the rail by a drowning man.

That February morning my father, in his untucked plaid shirt—perhaps his pajama top—and his work boots with soles flapping, struggled into a worn corduroy car coat and picked his way out to the irregular strip of sinking yard. By chance I looked up from where I was writing, rewriting actually, an essay for English 9 on *Gatsby*. The creek was glazed in early sun, a golden blue blur, where smudged clouds let the light through in patches that stained the water, soaked into the current, and disappeared.

Dad paced east and west along what I realized suddenly was more than a minor irregularity. No wonder Mom was bugging him. The actual scar created a deep brown gash in a sea of smashed green, as if some half-drunk giant had drawn its finger along the earth, thick and smudged and untoward. Even from my distant window it was ugly.

When the laptop blanked out, the flicker and flump from white to black snapped me back to the essay. *The Great Gatsby*, of course, is the morality tale best suited to baby-boomers' children. To want more creates moral havoc. It arouses the best and worst in humans. I'd read *Gatsby* three times. What stuck with me was a visceral connection to Nick and a lingering empathy with Daisy, who won't let herself have what she wants, fearful of her own ability to make the right choice, a teenage conundrum I recognized.

Without any assistance from Cliff Notes or Mr. Tedesco, our English teacher, I understood that Gatsby himself was not to be admired or pitied. He'd chosen his path with rabid determination, a path that upset the natural social order for purely selfish reasons. And Fitzgerald made it clear with every scene that Gatsby would get his just desserts.

One snowy afternoon my father had seen me reading the book and brightened visibly. "Ah-hah. I'm relieved to see they're still encouraging you to read the classics."

"It's required actually."

"Even better," he said as if the school department had finally heeded his personal recommendation. He cleared his throat and revived a rusty version of his first-year lecture on Fitzgerald, complete with one Napoleonic hand in his bathrobe in pedagogical splendor. The glimpse it offered of my father's brilliance saddened me. At Mom's insistent call from the kitchen, he deflated instantly and I felt very wise and grown-up. A feeling that didn't last.

His head-on attack of the seawall issues raised an immediate and surprised respect from me. A pad stuck out of one pocket and Mom's beat-up point-and-shoot camera swung from one hand. His head cocked in a way I connected with a hazy memory of PawPaw Gene at a bonfire, the same coat or one very similar and the same expression of intense concentration on the mystery before him.

There were no other faces in that memory. I had no idea when or where it had happened. PawPaw's brow glistened with a sheen of perspiration, the heat from the two-story fire an effusive flush even after the passage of time. He'd been dead a year by then. Although the coat might not have been a hand-me-down, the sleeves hung below Dad's wrists. Like a great sack the whole thing weighed him down, a tether to the ground as if he was too ethereal on his own to stay earthbound.

The original seawall, two or three years old that winter, had been built incorrectly by a contractor Dad met through AA. With children in Kansas or Oklahoma, some exotic place with cowboys and horses, the guy needed money for child support. My father was a sucker for stories about guys trying to do right by their kids. I knew all this from overheard arguments between my parents, in the way children stitch together reality like they force pieces into preschool puzzles, askew or overlapped with a fight-to-the-death conviction it is absolutely perfect and correct.

While I hadn't paid much attention to the original construction, the mounds of displaced dirt had provided fantastic slopes for mountain bike slides. Thirteen, stuck in hated middle school, I drove into the piles at high speeds with my friends in classic wing formation, a kind of death wish. When the front wheels bogged down, we twisted sideways and the bikes slid in satisfying 90-degree angles back to the yard in slow motion. A teenage version of mud pies. Once we were exhausted from repeated forays, Mom insisted we use the outside shower, even though it was November. I was embarrassed, but my friends shrieked with delight when we had to run back to the house, towels wadded over our private parts and bare-assed to the world.

The day of Dad's ditch investigation my mother was nowhere in sight, probably a purposeful evasion by him after their closed-door arguments. After taking photos, he stretched the tape measure outside the ditch and jotted figures on the pad. With each measurement he shoved the pad back in his pocket and replaced the pen behind his ear like a professional Hollywood carpenter. I was impressed. My father was not generally a handy man.

At one point he lay down on the seawall and took photos from the water side, his two feet splayed and hooked under the top board to keep from falling in. What he intended to do with the information I had no idea. He avoided controversy like most Catholics avoid the sanctuary on weekdays.

"I don't want to argue," he'd say to Mom when she started in.

"It's just a discussion, Eugene," she'd reply in her best Sunday school teacher voice.

And he'd bury his head in the newspaper so that she couldn't see his face. I figured he was smiling at the deflection.

By the time he scoured every AA meeting in a six-county area and failed to locate the original contractor, he had compiled a new list, glowing endorsements for each from a fellow recovering alcoholic. That's what they called themselves. The blatant admission struck me as a necessary prop, a string on the finger. It shoved the slim shadow of whiskey temptation back behind the steel gate of vocalized warning.

It was not until April that he began calling the names from our landline. The conversations rose in the stairwell like campfire smoke. Dad introduced himself, struck an early chord of camaraderie mentioning AA, and asked politely if they had time to take a look. Some phone calls ended abruptly. Perhaps, on principle, they simply didn't want to deal with another unreliable drunk. Several agreed to come but never showed. And several came and left without providing an estimate. My mother complained daily.

"The ditch is deeper. We could lose the yard altogether. Do you know how much fill dirt costs?"

"Beatrice, I get it, I do. But these guys are businessmen. They have to feel comfortable with the job. And they have to fit us into their schedule. The last thing we want is someone who doesn't know what he's doing or makes promises he can't keep."

"We already did that," she said bitterly.

It wasn't the money with Mom, though the cost was a lot of what they argued about, even before they knew what the repair would run. Her salary as the nursing home nutritionist barely covered the regular bills. With all my fifteen years of insight and worldly experience I was convinced what disturbed her most was the possibility that Dad and the new contractor would become buddies, and the repair would stretch out over months instead of weeks. My father craved an audience. And after he lost his university post, AA was his primary, if not only, outlet.

Mr. Robert J. Randle arrived in his bright red truck in early June. The twin to Dad's pad poked out of his shirt pocket, an answering pencil behind his ear. He looked reliable; his worn denim shirt with the sleeves rolled up advertised a workmanlike mind-set.

"Ah, here he is, the man of the hour," Dad announced in his most cheerful voice.

Without speaking Mom put her hand on my shoulder, her signal, *leave this to your father.* Although I wanted to watch him in action—he so rarely took charge—I understood the warning. Dad didn't need more pressure by having his son as an observer.

"The trash needs to go out," I said, not really asking.

Her nod echoed the entire unspoken instructions. *Fine but stay away from your father, come right back, don't mess this up.*

The two men shook hands and ambled toward the river, as if they were plotting golf putts and not rescuing our yard from the ravages of nature. And faulty workmanship. Mr. Randle took notes. He and Dad peered and knelt and measured, careful to stay off the top boards, twisted unnaturally under the pressure of the first contractor's mistakes and the tides. Whatever deal Mr. Randle and my father struck it was sealed with a formidable handshake and a tip of Mr. Randle's baseball cap. Dad didn't return to the house until the red truck had disappeared.

"Well?" Mom said, the empty plastic laundry basket gripped across her belly like a shield while Dad shrugged out of his boots.

"He knows what he's doing."

"Knows or sounds like he knows? When does he start?"

"Monday."

"Why not tomorrow? Didn't he think this was urgent?"

"Bea, I thought we agreed you were going to leave this to me."

When she didn't dispute that, my kid's brain assumed she was conceding. Another reality warp adults never fall into. Silence has many meanings but rarely does it stand for unanimity.

Mr. Randle wasn't gone fifteen minutes when our neighbor steamed through the break in the forsythia bushes and poked his head into the kitchen. Dad and I were watching a rerun of *The Rifleman* program, a pretty common Saturday morning activity. The routine started when my brothers were on college breaks, when Dad was trying to distract me from their mumbled debates upstairs about who had the shower first and who had insisted on the last round of tequila shots.

"Good morning, Eugene." Mr. Schoenberg's grin was schmarmy, over-the-top obnoxious. "Rory." I was clearly afterthought.

The Schoenbergs were weekend people. Fridays they fled Baltimore for the river but reported in endless detail all the social and cultural events they were missing. In animated enthusiasm, they gardened and swam and carried their wine glasses around the yard from morning to night. Luckily the ravine that dipped between the two yards discouraged the Schoenbergs from more than shouting most days. They invited my parents for cocktails or dinner by hallooing across the void.

Whenever the Schoenbergs came outside, my mother pretended not to hear or hid inside. Mr. Schoenberg's intrusions into our house without knocking irritated them both. But despite her rants, Dad kept backing down from telling him to stop. This Saturday was no exception. My father, his head bent to the crossword, ignored Mr. Schoenberg, looming in the doorway.

"Eugene." Mr. Schoenberg's voice conveyed a lifetime of chairing corporate board meetings.

"Richard," Dad acknowledged.

"We saw the red truck." Mr. Schoenberg waited. "So you've made arrangements about the wall?"

Dad nodded, still alternately eyeing the newspaper and the television where the bad guy—black leather vest, dented Stetson—had the Rifleman pinned to a fake boulder. When Dad grimaced sympathetically, I wasn't sure whether it was for the lawman or himself.

Mr. Schoenberg pushed. "He can fix our wall at the same time?"

Coordination of the repair had been discussed during the last year, though my parents thought it was a mistake. The same now-invisible contractor from AA had built the Schoenberg's existing wall and the same ditching was apparent in their yard. Mr. Schoenberg took great pleasure in beginning every conversational attack by reciting the current state of the damages. His gold signet ring with the Harvard crest flashed emphatically. Like the fox in *Little Red Riding Hood*, he grinned as he pointed at the leaning poles and enumerated the growing gap between the lawn and the wooden sheeting.

My parents hired an engineer early on, because, while the Schoenbergs had agreed to share the expense, they had dragged their feet. Not since the very beginning had they apologized for their drainage system's contribution to the wall failure. Lately they seemed to have forgotten their pipes continued to pour destructive volumes of water on the wall, exacerbating the "issues."

With the engineering report delivered and the remediation plan imminent, my father's urgent phone messages were mostly ignored by the Schoenbergs, as if they only remembered the "issues" when they could physically see them. It might've been different if they had been present for the first official report, the engineer's long jolly laugh as if he were delivering an unexpected birthday present.

"Too short, the damn poles, the sheeting, they're all simply too short."

My parents retreated to the bedroom. They argued loudly for long enough that I went for a run. When I returned, they weren't speaking to each other. It lasted through two Saturday confessions at St. Mark's, the longest my mother ever withheld her opinion.

When Mr. Schoenberg stepped over the threshold, Dad put down the newspaper. And the pencil. He swiveled in the chair.

"Yes, the red truck is our contractor. No, we did not discuss your wall. As I explained last weekend the engineer says the walls never should have been connected. Our contractor is going to install a new return wall and you can repair yours as you wish, with your own return wall."

Mr. Schoenberg whipped a rolled set of drawings from his back pocket with the flourish of pirate's sword from scabbard. "In my university engineering program—"

"Richard."

"Dick, please."

"Dick," my father repeated with a very different inflection.

I stifled a laugh at the imagined repartee from my brothers over the aptness of the name. My father's face was deadpan, his eyes blank, as if he had no opinion on the issue himself. He continued to speak with his eyes focused on the window.

"Mr. Randle will work on our wall for a period of time. It's a big job. Unfortunately. Feel free to approach him about your repair. But the walls will not be joined. It is part of the ongoing . . . issue." Said with no small degree of sarcasm.

"You don't seem to understand—"

"That's precisely why I hired the engineer."

"But we're neighbors. We share the riverfront. It's wasteful to each build an extra twelve feet of return wall. Extra poles, sheeting, fill. When we could just run the line."

"Expense is the least of my worries. We have standing water in our yard. We're losing dirt. With summer coming, the tides are only going to get higher. Your runoff continues to push against our wall." He took a deep breath. "We're out of time."

I could almost hear my mother cheer from her upstairs hiding place. Mr. Schoenberg stepped closer and pulled out a chair. He hadn't heard a word my father said.

My father's hands shook when he stood, and I held my breath, afraid he was going to deck Mr. Schoenberg. But when Dad spoke—finally—his voice was steady.

"I have work to do." And he marched out with more purpose than I'd seen him muster since he'd stopped teaching.

Mr. Schoenberg's gaze shifted. I buried my head in the puzzle. When I looked up, after scribbling in the seven letter word for "a ditzy person," he was gone.

"Airhead," I repeated to myself.

* * * *

The next Monday Mr. Randle trucked in his tools, gas cans, and hoses. He unloaded in a great hurry and left. An hour later a large delivery of planks and poles was loaded off, halfway between the house and the wall. When the red truck returned, he was pulling a flatbed with a scarred Caterpillar. Mud caked the treads like layers of a science fair topographical map project.

My biology book lay open on the desk. Crimson muscle flexed over sepia bone, nerve endings burst in firework blue. To the grind of heavy equipment I catalogued and memorized and reread the practice questions. To this day whenever I cut myself I see the gouged earth of our backyard after Randle opened it up that day.

He became Randle to all of us, though it was Mr. Schoenberg's abbreviation, as if the title Mister had not yet been earned. My mother, when she wasn't working, brought him cheese and tomato sandwiches. Dad left him encouraging notes, pinned on the lumber under whatever tool or half-drunk

Gatorade was within reach. "Looks great. Making progress" Two weeks into it, Randle was hard at work.

When I dragged off the late bus, weary from track practice, Randle and my father would be deep in conversation, each with a foot on the pile of unused poles, elbows on knees, hunched over the engineer's drawings, which Dad had sleeved in plastic to keep them dry. From the garage I could observe unseen.

If I started across the yard, though, they would straighten up—Randle to the earth mover or his truck cab, my father to the house—and there would be nothing more to hear. If Mr. Schoenberg appeared from the ravine, they also fled. It wasn't so much that they didn't like being caught jawing, but I suspected they didn't want the things they talked about overheard or repeated.

"Halloo," Mrs. Schoenberg vibratoed across the ravine one Saturday to my mother who was hanging boxers on the line in symmetry, three big boxers, one little boxer, three big boxers, one little boxer. Even though it was only Mrs. Schoenberg, it was embarrassing how skinny I was at fifteen and how little difference there was between my father and my sturdy brothers despite the age gap. I wished we were installing a perimeter fence instead of a seawall.

Mom waved without turning her head. Her mouth was full of clothespins; her apron from breakfast still stretched across her tummy in a wide band of Mardi Gras colors.

"Could I bring Randle lunch today?" Mrs. Schoenberg repeated. And when she received no answer, she raised her voice. "To save you the duty for once."

How, I thought, could she not understand my mother considered lunch an investment in our wall, her contribution? If she could keep on Randle's good side, he would do right by the wall, a moral quid pro quo. Mrs. Schoenberg's idea of duty, though, imposed a flavor to the relationship that almost guaranteed Randle wouldn't stay. My mother flung the clothespins into the basket on top of the wet laundry and started down the ravine at a clip that looked more like jogging.

Her hands gestured, wide and expansive at first, fist clenched against her palm for emphasis by the end. Mrs.

31

Schoenberg backed up the steps and was inside the door by the time my mother turned to tackle the incline home. Until Randle's little red truck bounced away at dinnertime, Mrs. Schoenberg didn't come outside again, though her pale face, without her characteristic neon smile, floated in their kitchen window. Later I realized why she seemed so ghost-like, the absence of the usual 1950's cherry lipstick on those tight lips.

* * * *

At first Randle worked every day. Or at least he was there when I trudged out to the bus stop and there when I returned in the afternoon. By the last week of school he'd adopted a new habit. In the drizzle he sat on the unused poles, his muddy boots like lollipops at the end of his overalls, the plasticized plans in his lap like a picture book. Early on my mother had wondered out loud why God would send such a small man to do this big job. When Dad muttered something about David and Goliath, she backed off. From the discouraged slope of Randle's shoulders that rainy day, he may never have heard the story.

"Hiya, Mister Randle. Rain's not helping, huh?"

He waved the plans. "It's the damnest thing."

"The drawings?"

"No, the creek. There's no bottom."

That sounded bad, and I wondered if he'd told my father. Rain soaked into my collar. I shifted the backpack to my head. Raindrops slid down my arm inside the windbreaker. Randle pulled his legs in and eased himself to standing.

"What did my dad say?"

"Call the engineer." Randle caught the exact tone of my father's exasperation as if ignorance was the culprit and not geology.

"What did the engineer say?"

"He doesn't return my calls."

We both stared at the fat new poles in the creek poking skyward just outside the failing wall. The tops stood uneven and battered where the vibrating head of Randle's heavy equipment had struggled to pound them down.

"It looks like a good start," I said with a purposeful dose of my father's optimism. It was not inherited.

"Deceptive. If you push through too far, you can explode the bottom. I'm afraid that's where we are."

"Explode the bottom? Like . . . literally blow it out so there's nothing there?"

Randle nodded, his misery as persistent as the drizzle. "All the way to China." He wriggled like a dog to shake off the rain, then eased into the truck.

"You're leaving?"

"I'm going to try and catch the engineer at his office."

But when he started the engine, my mother shot out the kitchen door.

"You're leaving? You were going to install the sheeting today."

"Tomorrow," Randle said.

"He needs to consult the engineer, Mom."

"But you said . . ."

The words trailed off even before Randle rolled up the window. My mother was a realist, perhaps a natural consequence of being married to an optimist who drank to disguise his own disappointment with reality.

We never saw Randle again or the little red truck. My father signed himself into rehab not long after that. Mrs. Schoenberg abruptly left off hallooing to my mother across the ravine, as if alcoholism might be contagious. And Mr. Schoenberg spent a whole Saturday without his wine glass, taking photos of the "issues," careful to stay on his side of the line. My brother, Frank, enlisted in the Marines and Danny moved in with his girlfriend. Speechless for once, my mother took up daily mass and paid me $2 a load to hang the laundry. The silence in the house was ominous.

Lonely and bored, I finished the entire summer reading list before July 4th. Although I debated whether to read *Gatsby* again, I chose instead *Things Fall Apart* by Achebe. Television had convinced me that Africa was the Wild West of the future. One stormy afternoon when I was bored with reading, my Dave Mathews accompanied by thunder and lightning, I discovered PawPaw's stiff canvas rucksack in a deep corner of the attic, the identification card filled out in his neat block letters. Cursive was not in the vocabulary of an economist.

His favorite Thoreau I'd heard him talk about so often was in the backpack, and there was a small slim volume, forest green with simple lettering. Robert Frost. Poetry. The publication page said 1916. The leather smelled musty, the corners worn. With the little book in hand, I pondered how the bag had ended up in our attic. PawPaw never lived here. My parents, still newlyweds, moved in when Dad took the university job, decades after PawPaw's legendary escape from poverty and ignorance, half a continent away from his father. I wondered at what point my father might have used his father's bag.

For decades the shadow of the legend divided them. Their reconciliation came only with PawPaw's first heart attack. The second one killed him five years later. Somewhere in that gap he must have handed off the bag and his son had accepted it, or at least used it to store a volume of poetry.

I scoured my memory for a scene with my father carrying the heavy pack. In elementary school Mom walked me home through campus on pleasant afternoons. By fourth grade my neighborhood friends and I often stopped to watch pickup games of soccer and Frisbee. Danny and Frank rode their bicycles into our heels, just to show off. Once in a while my father emerged from his office in his rumpled blazer and walked home with me. It made me feel grown-up, as if he chose me over my brothers because they couldn't appreciate what he had to say. It didn't occur to me then to wonder where he was on the other days, the times his chair at dinner was empty and he didn't come home until after I'd been banished to my room for homework or bed.

On our walks my father swung his battered briefcase by his side, the energy like a whistle to indicate he was happy, satisfied with his small world and his growing family. He talked about his students, odd questions of the day, wild excuses for lost homework or skipped reading assignments. He grilled me about geography and history, volunteered hints on public speaking and writing well. He tipped the front of my baseball cap affectionately and let his hand rest on my shoulder like we were colleagues. But the rucksack was not part of those memories.

Likewise I had not seen my father with the book of Frost's poems. He talked a lot about poetry, taught it in his American Lit classes, recited it when Mom gave him the cold shoulder for some offense or other. I'd never seen the small green volume.

And yet as I thumbed those pages, his voice rose up out of Frost's words. "Something there is that does not love a wall." And sitting cross-legged in the dusty attic I wished, for the first time in my life, for the world to turn backwards, for summer never to have come, for Mr. Randle to have stayed anonymous in his AA meetings. Even if I had to be back in middle school, I wished for my father to be once again the competent, organized fellow who had arranged for the seawall to be repaired, the optimist, the true son of my grandfather, the second coming, the legend.

One Owner

Becky Mushko

"I've brought my car in to be looked at." Wilma stood on tiptoes and watched the girl behind the window snap her gum and punch something into a computer. When the girl didn't look up, Wilma cleared her throat and tried again. "Excuse me," she said. "I've brought my car in to be looked at."

"Name?" the girl asked.

"Wilma Wright," Wilma said into the window. She watched the girl punch more computer keys. Why didn't the girl just forget about that contraption and give her more personal attention? It was only customer courtesy. "W-R-I-G-H-T," Wilma added. "Make sure you get it right."

The girl didn't get the pun—didn't crack a smile. She punched a few more keys and glared at the screen. Then she shifted her eyes back to Wilma. "So, you don't have an appointment?"

"Oh, no," Wilma said. "It's such a nice spring day that I thought I'd take the car out for a drive. I was going past and looking at all the redbuds in bloom along the highway when I saw your sign, and I—"

"So what's wrong with your car?"

"Oh, nothing really," Wilma said. "It's a fine car. I've had it for years. My late husband, Morton, bought it brand new. It's a one-owner car. Two, if you count me."

The girl snapped her gum and tried again. "So why didja bring your car to Carper's Car Palace?"

"I already told you," Wilma said. "I want it looked at. Like the sign out there says."

"Oh, right," the girl said. She punched some more keys. "It'll be awhile. We're kinda backed-up. Have a seat in the waiting room. One of the mechanics will take a look when he gets a chance." She pointed to the waiting area in the far corner.

"I left my car right in front of the door." Wilma pointed toward her 1979 white Impala. "The key's in the ignition. If that helps."

The girl didn't respond, so Wilma went into the waiting room. She helped herself to a complimentary cup of coffee and ensconced herself in a wingchair beside the fake fireplace. She picked up a magazine, thumbed through it, and put it back on the coffee table. A man sitting across from her reached for it.

"That's my car," Wilma said, pointing.

The man glanced out the window. "Nice." Then he turned his attention to the magazine.

A woman in a business suit came in and sat on the sofa. She opened her briefcase and took out some papers.

"Hello," Wilma said. "I brought my car to be looked at. It's right over there."

The business suit lady looked up from her papers to see the little white-haired lady watching her. "It's certainly in beautiful condition," she said, "for an antique. Did you restore it?"

"Antique! Oh, my, no! It's my car. I've always had it. Morton—he's my late husband—bought it brand new."

"Oh," the business suit lady said. "How nice." Then she busied herself with her papers and what Wilma supposed was one of those smart phones.

Several more people came and went. Wilma greeted each one and pointed to her car. After she'd waited two hours, Wilma saw a mechanic get into her car and drive it away. She waited another two hours, during which she had four cups of coffee, read three *People* magazines, and asked the girl where the restroom was. After Wilma exited the restroom, she poured herself another cup of coffee. She was halfway through another copy of *People* when a mechanic came out.

"Mrs. Wright?" he said.

"Yes."

"I've been all over your car. I've looked at the engine, the carburetor, the brakes, the electrical system, the tires—well, everything. I can't find a thing wrong with it. Your car is in excellent shape."

"I know," she said. "My late husband kept it in excellent condition and expected me to do the same. I rarely drive anymore, but I thought this would be a nice day for a drive. Then I saw the sign out front and decided the car deserved to be looked at."

"Well, I've looked it over pretty good," the mechanic said. "Did you notice any particular problems?"

Wilma thought for a moment. "Well, I've never really liked the color of the upholstery."

The mechanic suppressed a grin. "I'm afraid we don't do upholstery here. Your car is ready to go. Just go up front to the service counter. and they'll take care of you. Your keys are waiting for you there, and your car is right outside the door." He left before Wilma could say anything else.

She made her way to the service counter, which was on the other side of the room from where the gum-snapping girl was. A man was standing at the counter as if he'd been waiting just for her.

"That's my car," she said, pointing at the Impala. "If you'll just give me my keys, I'll be on my way."

The service manager put her keys on the counter and handed her a paper. "Do you want to pay this by cash, check, or credit card?" he asked.

Wilma looked at the paper. It said she owed over two hundred dollars.

"There must be a mistake," she said. "I only wanted my car looked at. I didn't authorize any work."

"This isn't for work," the man said. "It's for the mechanic's time and for the use of our testing equipment. Things like that."

"But I just wanted my car looked at! Like your sign says." Wilma pointed to the big sign out front: Bring your car here and let our mechanics have a look! "It's a beautiful car and doesn't get out much. I only wanted you folks to look at it—to admire it! I never in my wildest dreams thought you'd charge me an arm and a leg for the privilege."

"Ma'am? I'm not sure you understand—"

"Oh, I understand plenty!" Wilma crumpled the bill and tossed it onto the floor. "This is not a company that honors its word." She grabbed her keys and marched out.

Before the service manager could get to the door, Wilma sped off in her Impala. He picked up the bill and smoothed it out. Then he called his supervisor. "Got a minute, Joe? You aren't going to believe what this one owner just did."

Hidden Truth

Lois M. Holden

(First place fiction, *Skyline* Summer contest, 2016)

Hadley Armstrong limped toward the row of twenty or so mailboxes that formed a jagged line by the side of the road. The mile walk from his house was difficult on good days but almost impossible when the hot, humid air made it seem like he was trying to breathe underwater. The heat seemed to bother him more each year. This year's summer heat had arrived early and with a vengeance. He leaned against the first mailbox to catch his breath. His box was at the end of the row and Hadley noticed that it was leaning, almost touching Mrs. Cooper's box. Despite the pain, thinking of her made him walk faster as he made his way to his box. He managed a smile as he rubbed his hip, remembering his grandmother complaining about "the rheumatiz." However, his pain was a souvenir from Operation Desert Storm shrapnel along with a PTSD diagnosis and damaged lungs Hadley believed were caused by the Kuwaiti oil fires.

Mrs. Cooper's mailbox was empty but then it would be, as she had died two weeks earlier. He straightened up his box as best he could and opened the rusting, dented door. One hinge was missing and the door hung at a 45-degree angle. He had to reach through the woody vine that almost covered the entire box. The mail carrier had already left him a note that unless he repaired the mailbox and removed the vine, his mail delivery would be stopped. He didn't want to have to drive twenty miles to the post office, but he never seemed to think about it until he checked his mail. He pulled the vine away from the door as best he could, but the rest would have to wait until he brought nippers with him. Maybe when the weather cooled down he would get a new post and box. Hadley never expected much mail—some bills and an occasional flyer. Today he saw the electric bill and a dirty, smudged envelope. He thought, "probably an invitation to a gathering down at the river." Neighbors often ignored postal regulations and put mail in the boxes without postage.

He hoped there wouldn't be fireworks, as he couldn't stand loud noises like thunder or even people shouting. Another reminder of his military service. The Fourth of July celebratory fireworks at the river last year were almost more than he could take.

His wife, ex-wife now, learned to speak softly and never raise her voice to him. Hadley came back from the Gulf War a changed man. Almost anything, but especially loud sounds, would set him off. Sheila endured his bad temper and fits of rage as long as she could. Hadley was almost relieved when she divorced him. He found that living alone suited him well.

Passing Mrs. Cooper's box, he tried to put all thoughts of her out of his mind and started the trek back home. The sun was now overhead, beating down on his mostly bald head. Why hadn't he worn his hat? Then he remembered that he'd lost it down at the river while trying to pull in a catfish for his dinner.

Back at his house he pulled the mail from his overalls pocket, sat down at the table and looked at the electric bill. He blanched when he saw the amount due. Money was always tight and Hadley conserved every penny. He tried to stretch his disability check as far as he could. Not able to kick the nicotine habit, he rolled his own cigarettes. He cooked on a wood stove and heated his house with wood he cut from his property. About the only electricity he used was for the water pump and the house lights. He used the window air conditioner in his bedroom only on the hottest nights so he could sleep. Even then it was a struggle to pay his electric bill, especially since the rates had gone up again. To help ends meet, he collected scrap metal, but often that didn't even pay for his gas to drive to the scrap yard. Sighing, he opened the mystery envelope. He emitted a small scream, jumped up, and threw the letter down as if it had scorched him. After a minute, he sat down at the table and held his head in his hands. Stunned, he read the note again. "I saw what you did. For my silence, put $200 in small bills in the coffee can at the boat launch at midnight tonight."

His thoughts were a blur. "This must be a joke. No one could have seen me. I didn't mean to kill her. She was a nice old lady, if only she hadn't yelled at me. I was sure no one seen me. But someone did, and now they're gonna tell. I don't have no $200."

Mrs. Cooper was a widow about twenty years senior to Hadley, who had lived a mile down the road from him. She had had trouble getting around and walked with a cane. After her husband's death she fought with her daughter to stay in her home instead of moving to a retirement community. She thought of those places as just one step shy of the grave. She was able to handle most of the work around her house but often hired out odd jobs. She was proud of her garden and asked Hadley to do some cleanup work in her flower beds after a windstorm had strewn her garden with limbs and debris. He worked all morning, only stopping for smoke breaks.

Mrs. Cooper was a nice lady but had two very strong pet peeves: cigarettes and dirty floors. She hated cigarettes, because she blamed them for her husband's terminal lung cancer. She complained loudly when she smelled Hadley's cigarette smoke and saw the discarded butts on the ground. "Hadley Armstrong! You know better than to be smoking here on my property. You just pick up every last one of those butts. Don't let me catch you smoking here again!"

It had been a bad day for Hadley. Mrs. Cooper had been on him constantly about the quality of his work. His hips were killing him from the stooping, bending, and shoveling, so he took a break from the broiling sun and went into the house. He was getting a drink at the kitchen sink when Mrs. Cooper saw his footprints on her kitchen floor. "Hadley! First the cigarettes and now you've tracked mud all over my clean floor. You just get out of here now and don't expect me to pay you!" Her voice grated on Hadley's every last nerve. The slow-smoldering embers in his brain seemed to ignite. He usually tried to keep his temper under control but this day he exploded in a rage, lashing out at her. She quickly stepped back, but her cane slipped and she fell against the granite counter, hitting her head. Hadley ran to her, but he could see that she was dead. To keep from screaming, he shoved his fist into his mouth. "Oh,

41

God. Oh, God. What have I done? It was an accident but folks won't believe that, not after the whippin' I gave Cooter Jackson." He panicked, dragged her body over to the basement door, and pushed her down the stairs. He then cleaned up the blood on the counter, mopped up his footprints, and ran out the back door.

That was two weeks ago. Hadley had avoided all contact with his neighbors since then. Never a sociable man, he kept even more to himself and hadn't spoken to anyone since Mrs. Cooper's death. Her daughter, who found her body the next day, assumed her mother had fallen down the basement steps. There was no inquiry and Mrs. Cooper was laid to rest in the family cemetery plot. Hadley did not attend the funeral.

Now Hadley faced a dilemma. Someone had seen him leave the old lady's house. Even though he often did odd jobs for her, the timing of her death and his silence might look suspicious. Who could have seen him? And the bigger question was, where was he going to get $200? His disability check wouldn't arrive for another week and $200 would take a big chunk of it when it did arrive.

Hadley sat drinking coffee, thinking, and weighing his options. Touching a match to the letter and envelope, he made his decision. He prepared himself for the confrontation at the river. He didn't own a gun, but he often used a slingshot to kill rabbits and squirrels for his meals. His plan was surefire foolproof, he hoped.

That night was hot and humid. It didn't seem the air had cooled from the afternoon's heat. He arrived early at the river thankful for the full moon and cloudless sky. As he hunkered down in the tall grass next to the boat launch, he hoped his wheezing wouldn't alert the blackmailer to his presence. He did his best to ignore the swarm of mosquitoes buzzing around his head. In the bright moonlight he saw a figure approach the boat launch. Hadley didn't recognize him but watched as he looked around and crept over to the tin can that everyone used to hold fishing worms. He peered into the can, then stood up looking around. Hadley knew he had to act. A dead aim, Hadley took his slingshot, aimed for the temple and heard the satisfying thud as the rock hit home. He watched as the body tumbled into the water and was swept away. The river, swift from summer thunderstorms, soon carried the body out of sight. Hadley knew that the blow had either killed him outright or he was unconscious and would drown. Hadley felt strangely calm as if a great weight had been lifted from his shoulders. He made his way back home and slept a sweet, dreamless sleep.

Amelia Crockett was at her mailbox when he approached the next morning. Hadley nodded to her as he reached into his mailbox.

"Did you get one of those notes?" she asked.

"Whaddaya mean?"

"Oh, the 'I saw what you did' one."

"Did you get one, too?"

"Hell, Hadley, everybody did. After watching some old movie on the TV, Pete Johnson and Carl Pike wrote them and put them in everybody's boxes. Dumb kids. I thought you had to have some sense to get into college. Oh, well, I reckon they were bored and didn't have anything better to do. I suppose being out here on summer vacation is pretty calm after the excitement of a college campus. Carl told his mama this morning. He said Pete was going to check the can at the river last night—just in case. What an idiot! Good thing nobody out here has any secrets or they could have really stepped in it."

Reset

Phyllis A. Duncan

(First place fiction, Blue Ridge Writers Chapter contest, VWC, 2016)

It's looked on as child abuse today, but by the time I was eight or so, I could shoot a pistol and a rifle, and I could do so without managing to kill myself or anyone else.

One reason for that might have been I could shoot only when my father was home. He was in the Army, and we— my mother and I—didn't live on base with him. I'd pretend, though, using sticks and branches I found in the wooded area behind our house. Even then, I followed all his safety rules. This was in the days when I adored him, when every word he uttered was golden, and disobeying him was a sin.

I wasn't even nine when he bundled me in layers and layers of coats and socks and my snow boots and took me to Washington, D.C. On the way, I got a civics lesson about elections and how this country was different from the one he'd recently been stationed in, how every four years we could change our leader, and we didn't do it with tanks in the streets, but in voting booths.

A few months before that, he had taken me with him to the Baptist church in town—the First Baptist one where the good Baptists went, not the Second Baptist one where the sinning Baptists went. At school, Baptists of both persuasions had called my father—and me—a Papist. I didn't know what it meant, but I didn't like it.

With a sheet of paper and a pen in hand, he took me into a booth with a curtain across the opening. After he closed the curtain, he said, "This is a ballot. This is how we choose our government. Not everybody gets to do this, but in our country, everyone who is eligible to vote gets a say in how the country is run. It's called one man, one vote."

I wanted to know if women could vote, and he said, "Of course they can. Your mother will vote later. I wanted you and me to do this together, so you'll understand what to do when you're old enough."

He showed me each choice, explained who they were, who would get his vote, and why. This was the election where John Fitzgerald Kennedy, a Catholic like my father, won. My father had a thing for JFK, some of it about the religion issue but mainly to do with Kennedy's service in World War II.

"He had a rich father," he said, "and he could have bought his way out of serving, but he went to war anyway. He saved his men." That was enough to win my father's unswerving loyalty.

That would change, of course, over three years and civil rights.

Before that, though, on a frigid January, day he would put me on his shoulders so I could see an American president take an oath of office.

* * * *

Today, twelve-year-olds don't babysit. They're still considered babies themselves. But I started babysitting when I was eleven, watching toddlers and even infants. That pretty much convinced me not to have any children of my own, but I didn't quibble over the money I earned. The people I babysat for were so glad to have someone willing to watch their seven, stair-step brats, they paid me an outrageous amount for the time—$20 for Friday and Saturday nights.

My town had no bookstore, but it did have a drugstore with a book aisle. I'd pretty much exhausted the reading possibilities in the tiny local library, and twenty dollars a week got me a couple of paperbacks, a good supply of comic books, and sometimes a copy of *Time* or *Life* magazine.

My mother complained only when my reading material outgrew the top of my desk, and my father, out of the Army now, built a bookcase along one wall of my room, with shelves all the way to the ceiling.

He didn't raise an eyebrow about my choice of books until I came home with a thick paperback entitled, *The Rise and Fall of the Third Reich*, by William Shirer.

45

"There's a lot of bad stuff in there," he said. "If you get bothered, if you got questions, you ask me."

There was a lot of bad stuff, and I asked a lot of questions, ones he answered with reluctance.

That was how I learned my father also fought in World War II.

* * * *

I don't remember how much it cost then. Amazon will send me a well-used paperback version for $4.50, but that's at least three times more than what I paid. The public knew it as "The Warren Commission Report," but its official title was *The Report of the President's Commission on the Assassination of President Kennedy.*

It was almost as thick as the Shirer paperback, and I devoured it as quickly as I had *Rise and Fall.* One day I noticed it missing from the bookshelf, and I found my father in his recliner, reading glasses on, the Warren Commission Report open before him. Though he was the one to inspire my love of reading—he read three newspapers a day, numerous agriculture magazines and books, and Civil War histories—he was a much slower reader. Over the next few weeks, I caught him reading the Warren Report, and on occasion he would take from his shirt pocket a small, spiral-bound notepad and the pencil he sharpened with his pocket knife and make notes.

He kept important notations in that little book: what mixture of fertilizer in which field; which fields would be planted and which would be fallow next season; when the cows were bred, so he could calculate their due dates; how many rows of corn had gone through the combine's head, so he'd know when to do maintenance; and, apparently, notes on the Warren Commission Report.

When he finished the book and returned it to my room, I—Nancy Drew fan that I was—went through the paperback for clues to see what had fascinated him, but he'd put not so much as a pencil mark in any margin.

* * * *

One Sunday morning, while my mother and my little brother, a recent arrival but quickly becoming a pain in the ass, still slept, my father woke me.

"Dress warm," he said, "and meet me at the office."

His farm office was a tool-lined room in the equipment barn. There was a wood-burning stove, a small desk, and a coffeemaker. He always took a thermos from the house but made his own pots throughout the day in his office. His filing system was a series of shoe boxes, labeled with the year, on shelves. Ask him for a record of some purchase from three years before, and he could put his hands on it within seconds.

When I walked in and closed the door behind me, I saw his dog, the one he always wanted to ride in the truck with him but that always managed to disappear when the truck door opened, curled up before the stove. He quirked his ears at me and wagged his tail, but Sam was a laid-back dog who didn't like to stir much from his warm spot. That room was always warm, redolent with burning pine, and I would sometimes hide there, knowing my mother would never darken the doorway.

Two things out of the ordinary I noticed right away. A pumpkin from the garden sat on the floor just inside the door, and my father's Remington bolt-action rifle, with scope, leaned against the scrap metal bin.

Glasses balanced on the end of his Roman nose, my father was flipping through some pages in his notebook.

"Would you say that punkin is about the size of a man's head?" he asked me, not looking up.

I studied it, and since the only man's head I knew was his, I compared the two. "Yes, sir," I said. "What are you gonna do with it?"

"You'll see. Go start the truck. Let it warm up," he said.

"Can I carry the Remington?" I asked. "Can I shoot it?"

"No, I'm going to be doing the shooting today, but you can carry it to the truck. Remember how I told you: business end pointed toward the ground."

"Yes, sir."

I took the truck keys from the hook and picked up the Remington, tucking the stock in my armpit and letting the barrel rest on my forearm. I started the truck and slid over to the passenger side, holding the Remington so it wouldn't flop over when the truck moved.

My father got in the truck not long after, thermos under one arm and the pumpkin under the other. He set the pumpkin and the thermos on the seat between us, put the truck in gear, and drove off to a spot on the farm we called Hill Field, because of the hill bulging in the middle of it. In my mind it had been a dormant volcano, an Indian burial mound, and a mass grave of Civil War dead. Over the summer, almost every night I had climbed to its summit with the telescope I'd gotten the previous Christmas so I could stargaze.

My father put me at the base of the hill and handed me the end of his long tape measure. He took his notepad out and flipped to pages where I saw he'd made some drawings, triangles with numbers along the sides. He paced to the length of the tape measure, motioned me toward him, put me on the spot where the tape ended, paced away and measured again, and put me on that spot. He went back to the truck and drove to where I stood. He unloaded some hay bales and stacked them next to me. He used the tape measure to determine the height of the bales and added a few flakes of hay until he had the height he wanted. On top of the hay, he set the pumpkin.

He motioned me into the truck, and I held onto the Remington again before he reminded me.

Not too long ago there was some commercial for a pickup truck where it climbed a steep grade while some rival make and model couldn't make it. They could have filmed that commercial on that day in November 1964 when my father drove a decade-old Chevy pickup to the apex of Hill Field.

* * * *

My father sat in the truck and drank some of his coffee, offering me a taste. It was strong and black, with a little sugar, and when I took a sip, I realized that was part of the smells I always associated with him—coffee, cherry pipe tobacco, Old

Spice. When he was still in the Army and would have to go back after leave, I'd sometimes find a shirt of his in the dirty laundry and keep it under my pillow. Those smells meant there was someone in the world who loved me.

"What did you think of that Warren Commission Report?" he asked.

"It had a lot of details," I replied.

"Did you understand all of it?"

"Most of it. Some of it was gross, worse than those sections in Shirer's book about the concentration camps."

His face paled, or it was a trick of the light. I wasn't sure.

"Did you believe all of what you read in that report?" he asked me.

"Well, I guess so. There were all those big shots on the commission. Wouldn't they tell the truth?"

He gave a nod and drank more coffee. "Shooting's a skill you have to practice," he said, "like that guitar teacher of yours tells you to do after every lesson, like hitting a baseball, or throwing a football. To be a crack shot, you have to practice. You agree?"

I thought I did. I know he didn't go out and practice shooting at all. Every time he took me target shooting, he always shot bull's-eyes, but I said, "Yes, sir."

"Something in that Warren Report troubles me," my father said. "Do you remember the part where it said that Lee Oswald guy fired three rounds in four point eight to seven seconds?"

"Yes, sir."

"That rifle he used, the Carcano, it's an Eye-talian rifle, but it's similar to that Remington there you got. Now, the report says either the first or second shot missed. One shot hit the president in the back and came out the front of his throat. The final shot hit him in the head."

I remembered when I read that part in the book. I thought it would be like when people got shot on *Wagon Train* or *Bonanza*—no blood, no brains. The description in the report was graphic enough to give me nightmares. If I'd said anything, though, he and my mother would start looking at my reading material closer, and I didn't want that. I'd just discovered science fiction and horror.

"I remember," I said.

"I'm no expert shooter," he said, though I'd seen his Army marksmanship medals, "but it seems to me Oswald would be hard-pressed to get off three shots in seven seconds, much less four point eight. And if he did, I don't see how accurate they could be with a moving target. You know how to operate a stopwatch?"

"I think so."

He took one from his pocket. "You press the stem like this," he said, and pressed it with his thumb, "and it starts. To stop it, you press the stem again." He did that, and the racing hand on the watch halted. "Each of the longer hash marks is a second, the shorter ones in between a half-second. So, how many seconds does that read?"

I studied the watch face. "Four," I said.

"Good. You press this little button here on the side, and the hand goes back to zero. Got that?"

"Yes, sir. Daddy, what is it we're going to do?"

That smile he gave me is the one I remember, even now, fifty years later, the one that hovers in my memory like a ghost. After that day, his smile would come less and less. I can't for sure make the connection between his little experiment and his own death two decades later, except in hindsight, and even then it's not twenty-twenty.

"Now, this isn't exactly a scientific experiment because we don't have a moving target, but we're going to see if that Warren Commission Report can be believed," he said.

* * * *

When my childhood questions had delved into "What did you do in the war, Daddy?" his answers were always terse and sharp.

I knew he'd been in a tank. His tank fought other tanks, and I'd seen enough World War II movies by this point in my life that I knew it meant the tanks caught on fire and men would climb from them and stagger around burning.

Sometimes their *Kameraden* (I learned that word from the movies, too.) would shoot them to put them out of their misery. Maybe our guys did, too.

My father's tales of his time in the European Theater, as I later learned it was called, were antiseptic. All he ever said was something to the effect of, I got in my tank, I took it where I was told, I did what I was ordered to do, Hitler killed himself, and the war was over.

He had a few shrapnel scars, and there was the arthritis in five places in his spine where being crimped between two tanks broke vertebrae. That was during the Occupation, and he didn't get a Purple Heart. The shrapnel wounds, received in combat, he'd tended himself and that, too, meant no Purple Heart. Years later several pieces no bigger than peas worked their way through muscle and skin to pebble his forearm. Even then, he dunked his pocket knife in the disinfectant we used when we dehorned cattle, and excised them himself, covering the cuts with Band-Aids.

I had wanted to keep the sharp-edged pieces of metal, wet and bright with blood. I thought they would be cool to take to class and show everyone, but he took them from me and tossed them in the wood stove in his office.

* * * *

The front end of my father's farm pickup served as the ledge of the Texas School Book Depository sixth-floor window. In the Warren Commission Report, there was a picture of an FBI agent, or some such, crouched at the real window in the real Texas School Book Depository in a posture, which, the FBI concluded, Oswald must have used. My father approximated that posture and told me to get ready with the stopwatch. He would count down, he said: three, two, one, go! I was supposed to hit the stopwatch's stem on "go!" and hit it again after the last shot.

When someone would finally digitize the Zapruder film so you could see the bullet hit President Kennedy's head, see the pink spray of blood, brain, and bone, I would remember that day at the top of Hill Field when my father got off three rounds from a bolt action Remington rifle in 5.5 seconds. Two went into the hay bales, marked by eruptions of straw, and the third, like Oswald's, hit the pumpkin on the right rear side, sending an orange spray of skin, pulp, and seeds into the air.

When the pumpkin exploded, I may have whooped in triumph, and when I looked at the stopwatch's hand pointing to 5.5, I may have jumped up and down. But when I looked at my father, mouth ready to say, "You did it, Daddy! You did it!" I grew quiet. He gazed at the ruined pumpkin, but at the same time his eyes looked at something far away. He was there but not there, and I held my breath, not knowing what to do.

He stayed in that crouch so long, my own back ached from it. I saw the sunlight shine off tears on his cheeks, and I looked at the ground. When you're twelve and your daddy is your whole life, when he is the one who keeps the monsters at bay, it's too world-shattering to see him cry. After that, I would see him do it again. And again. Each successive time, I got angrier and angrier to the point where I wasn't even speaking to him when he died.

I heard the fabric of his clothes rustle as he straightened. He sniffed, hauled out his handkerchief, and blew his nose.

"What's the stopwatch say, Doll?" he asked.

"Five and a half," I said, still not wanting to look at him.

"Let me see," he said, and his rough, calloused palm came into view. I lay the stopwatch in it. "And you did it just the way I showed you?"

"Yes, sir."

"Well, damn," he said and slipped the stopwatch back into his coat pocket. He unloaded the Remington and handed me the rifle and the magazine box. "Get in the truck, and let's go get those hay bales."

We left the pumpkin for the groundhogs, a treat, my father called it. I wanted him to ask why I stared at the floorboard of the truck and grunted responses to his questions. I wanted him to, but I didn't have any answers.

Back at his office, he headed inside and told me to go to the house and put the rifle back in the cabinet. A long time later—months rather than weeks—I asked him if we could go shoot the aluminum cans I'd been collecting from the trash bin for days, but he shook his head.

"You're old enough to go do that on your own now," he said. "You know the rules, and I trust you."

The point was this was a thing we did together, standing side by side on the makeshift firing range, keeping score of how many cans we hit.

Not long after, adolescence took me full force, and boys started to be more interesting than plinking at cans with a twenty-two. We never shot together again.

Twenty years later, when I took it upon myself to clear the house of his presence so my mother wouldn't have to, I found the stopwatch in his nightstand. It still read 5.5, and that day came back with a clarity I've rarely had since. The smell of hay, of dirt, of pumpkin, of gunpowder, coffee, tobacco, Old Spice. The way the sunlight highlighted his tears, and would anything in the past few weeks have been different if I'd asked why he was crying?

I pressed the reset button on the stopwatch and returned it to zero.

Over the Moon

Deborah M. Prum

(Second place fiction, *Skyline* Summer contest, 2016)

Charlottesville, Virginia
August

Early that morning, before anyone else was awake, Maclain snuck into his mom and dad's room and peeked into the bassinette. He felt glad that baby Sudie did not look anything like his other sister who died. This one seemed lots smaller and had a round, red face and bunches of dark hair—that stand-up baby hair. This one screamed a lot. After supper last night, her little mouth looked like an angry "O." Maclain didn't remember if Eileen screamed that much. Honestly, he felt happy about Sudie's wailing. It meant she wasn't dead. She could wail all she wanted.

Mom and Dad had brought her home yesterday afternoon. They'd picked up Maclain from the Kristoff's home after leaving the hospital. Even though staying with the Kristoffs the night before meant Maclain could play with Tim all day, he hated being there. He missed living next to the Chappells in North Carolina, where all the kids had free run of the house and the field behind the house and did anything they wanted like have giant pillow fights or jump out of the barn loft onto bales of hay or secretly make campfires in the woods. At the Kristoffs the night before, they'd eaten kale and tofu and bread with chewy brown stuff in it for supper and then went straight to bed (quietly) after doing their homework.

Maclain could hardly see Sudie when he climbed into the back of their car. They'd wrapped her like a mummy in her car seat. All he got a glimpse of was her scrunched-up eyes and tiny nose. His dad said, "So what do you think? Here's our new baby."

"Can she breathe okay? Those blankets . . ." Maclain felt worried and not much else.

When Maclain first set eyes on his other baby sister,

Eileen, he remembered that he was so happy that he jumped up and down. He felt over the moon because now he wasn't alone anymore. He gave that other baby a card, which he still has, hidden in the bottom drawer of his bureau. It said, "Wellcom Home Baby Ileen—Yur Mine!" He was a much better speller now, but he didn't make a card for this new baby. He would never say it out loud, but he decided to wait; he needed to see if this baby wound up staying.

Somehow, he believed that Eileen's death had to be his fault. He never said that out loud either. But, in his heart, that's exactly how he felt. That bad morning, he should have gone to her room before he headed to school. He could have woken her up before she died and then she wouldn't be dead. He didn't tell anyone this—he didn't want them blaming him, but he knew it was his own fault. But he felt mad, too, mad because big old God, who could do anything he wanted anytime he wanted, also didn't bother to wake up Eileen that morning. Everybody told Maclain that God loved him and that he was supposed to love God, too, but mostly Maclain felt angry and scared of what God might let happen next.

The next morning Maclain woke up to Mama Jewell, Daddy Buck, and cousin Leenie in the house. They'd gotten in the night before, after Maclain had gone to bed. They'd taken the first available flight out of Dallas. No waiting around this time. Maclain clearly remembered Mama Jewell crying and crying at baby Eileen's funeral, saying she never even got to meet her granddaughter. They all were supposed to have flown East for Christmas, but Eileen didn't live that long.

He could hear them downstairs, Daddy Buck's low, rumbling laugh, cousin Leenie's happy voice that sounded more like someone singing a pretty song than just plain old words. He smelled bacon and coffee and maybe home fries. Mama Jewell, his grandmother, made the best breakfasts. Daddy Buck said he always needed to fuel up before he put in a full day of ranching. Maclain loved Daddy Buck, even though Daddy Buck wasn't exactly his real grandfather. He'd never met his real grandfather, Jack Maclain. Nobody talked about that grandfather except once when they were visiting Texas and he heard his Aunt Vee call Jack a "no count drunk politician who hightailed off rather than take care of his wife and baby." Maclain never brought up Jack, since he felt perfectly happy with Daddy Buck.

Maclain hadn't been in the kitchen one full second before Mama Jewell rushed toward him, arms wide open. "Let me get my hands on you, child." As she gathered him in, Maclain smelled that old familiar perfume she wore—a whiff of cinnamon cake and angels.

"Good Lord, you've grown a foot!" As Mama Jewell held him at arms' length to get a better look, cousin Leenie came up from behind and gave him a bear hug.

"Your hair's what's grown—*two* feet, I believe. Boy, you need yourself a cut." Leenie brushed her hand over his crew cut, which, he had to admit, was standing up pretty high. "Lucky for you I brought my scissors."

Cousin Leenie owned a beauty shop back in Texas. Dad joked that Leenie never traveled without her scissors. She was always after him, too. Dad never seemed to care that much about his looks. Maclain's mom said his dad got haircuts about three weeks after he really needed to.

Daddy Buck got up from his chair and lifted Maclain all the way up to the ceiling, "Here's my guy." Maclain felt that he might be too old to be lifted up that way, but he didn't mind so much because he liked Daddy Buck and felt great that Daddy Buck seemed crazy about him.

"Come on, partner, pull up a chair beside me. I got a special present for you." Daddy Buck lowered his huge self into a kitchen chair. Maclain always felt in awe of his size. A while ago when Mac's buddy, Theo, met Daddy Buck, he said, "Your grandpa is a walking mountain."

You wouldn't call Daddy Buck fat, but more like solid. Big solid head, neck, shoulders, hands. Maybe his stomach did pooch out a little, but he looked more like a superhero than an old fat person. Maclain always felt safe around him.

Daddy Buck checked through his blue jeans pockets, both in front and back, but finally found what he was looking for in his shirt pocket. He pulled out a small package, "Just for Mister Maclain. Every boy your age needs one. I already got parental approval, more or less." He winked at Mama Jewell, who raised her eyebrows.

His mother wasn't there to tell him to be polite, so Maclain tore right into the package. A silver pocketknife! Maclain's jaw dropped. He said, "No way! Mom and Dad said okay?"

"Well, yes, after some convincing and negotiating on rules." Daddy Buck looked at him, trying to be serious, but Maclain could see a tiny smile. "You've got to be responsible. You can't use this until I teach you how. I'll show you right after breakfast. Of course, you can't bring it to school or church or any place other than where I tell you. Remember, it's a tool not a toy."

True to his word, right after breakfast, Daddy Buck showed Maclain how to open and close the knife safely and how to whittle, always away from your body. He even showed him how to carve his initials in a piece of scrap wood. Of course, Daddy Buck went over the rules, too, which included not showing the knife to any friends or letting anyone play with it.

Now that last rule was a tough one for Maclain because he wanted so badly to show Tim the knife, to let Tim know that his family thought he was old enough to have his own knife. But Maclain knew Tim would want to play with the knife. Who wouldn't? And Mac also knew that he wouldn't be able to say "no" to Tim. So, he didn't say a word about it at school the next day.

Sudie cried her way through the next couple of days, waking up at least three times a night. One night the crying went on so long that Maclain crept out into the hallway and looked into his mother's room. He could see his dad holding Sudie, who still was screaming. Mama Jewell was hugging Maclain's mother who seemed to be crying just as hard as Sudie.

His mother kept saying, "I can't do this. There's something wrong with the baby. I know it. I can't go through . . ."

Mama Jewell didn't let his mother finish her sentence. "Andi, you've got to stop it. Right now. This baby has colic, no more, no less. And, you are overtired."

His mother cried harder. Mama Jewell held her for a good long time and then turned to Maclain's father. "Jacob, I'll take the baby. She's just nursed. She'll be fine. Get some sleep."

Mama Jewell walked past Maclain in the hallway. "Honey, get yourself back to bed. Right now."

But Maclain didn't go straight back to bed. Instead he looked down through the banister into the family room. Mama Jewell sat in a rocker with baby Sudie across her lap, patting her on the back, not little pats but firm ones. After a while, Sudie stopped crying and seemed to fall asleep. Maclain must have fallen asleep, too, because later he felt Mama Jewell half-carrying, half-walking him back to bed.

Daddy Buck, Mama Jewell, and cousin Leenie stayed a full week. Everybody got a haircut from Leenie, even Tim, who happened to come by one day. Well, Sudie didn't get a haircut, although, in Maclain's opinion, she needed one. Her hair grew straight up and slanty, like some kind of punk rocker, but everyone thought she looked cute that way.

Mama Jewell cooked lots of food, enough for Maclain's scout troop to eat there for a few weeks. She put the meals in the freezer. On their last night, Mama Jewell made all of Maclain's favorites: barbeque, chow chow, and Texas sheet cake. After Eileen died, his mom had taken a little break from cooking real food. Maclain didn't mind the Tater Tots and fish sticks so much, especially if he had plenty of ketchup, but Mama Jewell's cooking made his insides way happier.

The first few days after Sudie came home, his mother kept her in a bassinette right by her side all day and all the time—in the kitchen, the living room, even in the bathroom while she took a shower. Mama Jewell convinced his mother that Sudie couldn't sleep well with all that moving around. She talked her into letting the baby nap in a quiet, dark room. So, by the end of the week, Sudie seemed to have calmed down. Maclain's mom and dad didn't seem as jumpy, either.

Maclain went along when his dad drove them out to the airport. Daddy Buck and Mama Jewell gave him a sandwich bear hug—that is a big hug where you get completely squished between two people. Once again, Maclain knew he was too darn old for sandwich bear hugs, he didn't mind it at all and just wished they would stay longer. Leenie kissed his forehead. Then they all dragged their suitcases through security, waving and saying good-bye as they went. Maclain tried to hold back his tears, but let a few slip anyway.

Over the next few weeks, Maclain watched Sudie as she grew and changed each day. Her hair flattened out and started to look normal. Maclain couldn't help but like how cuddly she felt and how he could hold the whole of her in his arms. He loved the way the top of her head smelled after her bath and how she grabbed his finger. Yet, part of him fought against getting too close to the baby. If someone were to ask him, he couldn't name the feeling but he knew it was there.

One night, Daddy Buck telephoned Maclain. Maclain loved when he did that. Daddy Buck just plain made him feel special and important. After talking about school and basketball and nothing much, Daddy Buck asked, "Well, how's your baby sister?"

Maclain couldn't say why, but when he heard the question, he immediately thought of Eileen and was about to say, "Dead. She's dead. Daddy Buck you know that."

But Maclain stopped himself, realizing Daddy Buck was talking about Sudie, the living, kicking, smiling baby sister. "She seems to be fine . . ." Maclain hesitated.

"What is it, son?"

Maclain felt on the verge of tears, he struggled to control his voice. "Do you think Sudie will die, too?"

Daddy Buck didn't answer right away. In fact, Maclain wondered if the line had gone dead.

"That is a hard question. I want to give you an honest answer and that is I don't know. I don't think so, but I don't know. Hell, I don't know if I'm going to live to tomorrow."

Maclain sighed. "Daddy Buck, that doesn't make me feel any better."

"Well, I'm sorry but I never want to lie to you, Mac."

Maclain stayed silent a few seconds, thinking about Sudie. "It's hard. I'm scared."

Daddy Buck continued, "I know. It is scary. Here's how I see it. When you let yourself love somebody, you open yourself up to a world of pain and the possibility of someday losing what you dearly love. But what's the alternative? Rolling up in a ball and dying. I'd choose loving every time."

A week or so later, on a Sunday afternoon, Maclain asked his father if he could whittle in the backyard. His father happened to be reading and said yes without looking up. Even though Maclain felt certain his father hadn't paid any attention to his question, he headed outside with his sliver pocketknife. He found a tree near the far edge of their yard, near the top of the meadow. He carefully unclasped the knife exactly the way Daddy Buck had shown him.

Then, slowly, he began to carve "SUDI" into the trunk of the tree. The letters looked all slanty. In fact, the "S" in Sudie looked more like a "5." After he finished digging out the letters, he cut the shape of a heart around them, quite lopsided, but more or less recognizable as a heart.

When Maclain finished, he realized he'd left off the "E" in Sudie's name, but if he carved it in now, he'd have to place the letter outside of the heart, which he didn't want to do. Instead, he dug out a much bigger heart all around the outside of the first one. He added the "E" at the end of SUDIE but then used that same "E" to start the name "EILEEN" dropping down along the inner edge of the larger second heart. Just as he finished the last "N" in Eileen's name, the knife slipped and he cut his left thumb, not too deep, but enough to bleed. A steady trickle ran down his hand toward his wrist.

Maclain wiped his hand on the back of his jeans. He hoped his mother wouldn't notice the stain. His finger started to ache a bit. Maclain remembered what Daddy Buck had said about how loving somebody could bring a world of pain. What did that mean? Maybe it's that when you love somebody, happiness and sadness gets all mixed up inside of you. Since Eileen died, he'd only been feeling sadness. Maybe if he let go of some of the sadness, he could make room for just a little happiness.

Maclain stood back and looked at the tree: Eileen's and Sudie's names mixed together, with a big heart around both of them. He thought, "Maybe I made a mistake, but it now looks

60

exactly the way it should be."

Transgression

J. Elizabeth Vincent

(Second place fiction, Blue Ridge Writers Chapter contest, VWC, 2016)

Sunlight touched me. It somehow fought its way down through the pointed jade treetops to warm me. It played along my bare, bruised skin, brushed its fingers through my long, tangled hair. I felt my being melt, dissolve into a million tiny motes.

I let go of my forced stillness and rose from the ground in pieces. I floated along the rough edges of tree bark and slithered between slick, shaded needles, up, always up, toward the halo of burning white. That was where I had come from, where I was ready to return.

When the crunching and rustling of leaves shattered the silence, I fought not to focus on it, to pretend that it was only the wind, but the rush of water below, echoing off the cliff faces, became louder. And I began to sink. Desperate to reach the light, I fought, tried to claw my way up, but instead of air or treetops, I felt only cool soil push itself under my fingernails.

The deep tenor of his voiced grabbed me, pulled me down, and slammed me back into my body, back into its pitiful mass. I heard the sound of a zipper being pulled along its teeth. It grated along my nerves like broken glass.

His face, looming above me, blocked the light.

"Come on. Get moving. I want to reach the lookout by lunchtime."

His stinging slap on my thigh and the sharp rock cutting into my back reminded me that there was never any escape. The light was not meant for me.

Although I couldn't move quickly, I sat up and began gathering my clothes from the leafy bed below me. I shook each piece before I dressed, not because I cared but because he did.

Everything hurt, especially when I gingerly settled my panties into place. I tried to ignore the bruises on my thighs.

Some were yellowish, but some were still red, just blooming on my white skin. I'd spent hours staring at bruises like these, fascinated by their progression. I'd gotten to the point where I could figure out when they would fade almost to the day, when it would be safe to wear shorts or a short-sleeved shirt again.

"Katherine, do I have to drag you up this trail?" Andrew's pack was settled on his back, and he stood directly in front of me.

"I'm almost ready." I pulled up my jeans, refusing to meet his gaze. I didn't want to see his face, afraid that I'd find either a knowing smirk or anger in his eyes. Most of all, I didn't want to chance that I'd see tenderness there. There was often tenderness after he hurt me. Sometimes, he would even apologize.

He started moving before I had slipped my boots back on. I had no idea where we were really, just that we were hiking upward along the banks of the Delaware. So, I hopped up the trail, trying to get my last boot on with one hand while trying to put my backpack on with the other. I almost asked him to wait, but instead, I bit my tongue and struggled along behind him.

* * * *

It had been at least ten minutes since I'd last seen Andrew's back, his knit yellow shirt, and his sandy hair. He'd kept hiking at a good pace, never looking back. He must have reached the overlook by now.

He would expect me to be there soon, but I chanced a short break, only a few seconds, to catch my breath. There was another steep incline waiting in front of me. I glanced back down the trail, but I was all alone. I looked around. The brush got thicker away from the trail, and I wondered how long it would take for a person to get lost in there. Could I get away from the trail quickly and still leave no trace?

Don't ever even think about leaving me. You'd never survive on your own.

Andrew was right. He was better than I was. He would find me. He would punish me. I wasn't the good wife he deserved, but he'd put up with me. He'd taken care of me.

Dragging one foot in front of the other, I started moving again. I wished I could go back up into the air, away from myself, away from the pain. I'd never be good enough for him. I was always failing.

* * * *

Andrew was waiting at the top of the trail. He was still so handsome. As handsome as the day I'd met him at my father's church. There was a little grassy inlet to the left of the trail where he'd thrown his backpack. He stood there, leaning against the cliff, his muscular arms folded against his chest.

I waited for him to say something as I approached, so I could gauge his mood.

"Hurry up, Katie," he said. "You've got to see the view."

Katie. I looked up at his face. He was smiling, the dimple on his tanned cheek deepened. I tried to smile back.

"Here . . . here. Put your backpack down." He grabbed it from me and dropped it beside his.

Clasping my hand, he pulled me to the other side of the trail, where the trees opened up. I gasped and stopped walking as the earth opened up about ten feet in front of me, dropping away to the river below. Its roaring waters had quieted to a mere murmur, and its surface looked like green glass.

"Go closer," he whispered in my ear. He had moved behind me. "You can't really get a feel for it unless you're on the edge."

"No! Andrew, I can't! I'm scared!"

"Don't be a baby. Just look," he said. He was already pushing me. His hands on my shoulders and the pressure of his chest on my back inched me slowly forward.

"Andrew!" My voice came out in a high squeak.

I tried to dig my heels in, but against his strength, I was nothing. "Please, please, Andrew . . ."

My eyes were glued to the ground. When I saw the gravel and dirt start to drop away before me, I panicked and spun around. I grabbed at Andrew's shirt for support. My legs slid out from under me. The yellow fabric was ripped from my grasp. My whole body slapped the ground. Tiny rocks scraped my cheek and my hands. The cuts burned.

I began to sob. "I'm sorry, Andrew. Please, don't make me look. Please."

I folded my arms over my head and waited for his scream, waited for the blow to come. But except for the soft patter of gravel on the rocks below and the murmur of the river, the forest was quiet. I waited, but still, there was no sound.

* * * *

Slowly, I lifted my head, looked out through my hair. I was alone. "Andrew?"

I sat up and looked around. He was gone. Our backpacks still lay in the grass several yards away. "Andrew?" I said more loudly. I could hear the quiver in my voice.

Climbing to my feet, I turned around. I could see handprints on the ground where I had fallen, the impression that my body had made in the dirt. Behind it, there were more marks, boot prints and what looked like skid marks.

My heart suddenly sped up, and my chest tightened. "Andrew," I croaked.

I dropped onto my hands and knees and scrambled to the edge of the cliff. It fell down in an uneven jumble to the river. I saw a wide smear of blood on a boulder about twenty feet down. Further down, I saw a boot lying on a rock close to the water's edge. But he was gone.

"Andrew!" I screamed.

I screamed and screamed until my voice was hoarse. But I already knew that my husband, my everything, would never be able to hear my voice again.

What had I done?

Snake Bit

Jack Trammell

(Third place fiction, *Skyline* Summer contest, 2016)

Colson tried to wiggle his feet in the bottom of the sleeping bag and felt a response. But it was not the response he had hoped for. It was delayed and confused, as if his feet didn't know what he wanted them to do. The right one was increasingly numb. About calf level was lightning hot pain.

He moaned and shot his head out of the sleeping bag. It was a cool night, but he was burning up alive.

"Hurry up, Elroy!" he said out loud, grunting for oxygen. "Hurry up, for God's sake!"

Somewhere further down the mountain, Elroy had gone for help. They both knew that a bite from the Eastern Diamondback, "The King," as it was known locally, was far more dangerous and potentially deadly than the copperhead or other types. Colson closed his eyes and tried not to worry.

Even so, his head was filled with heavy, unshakable thoughts: He was to be married in a month. He was to go to Richmond next week to meet his brother. He had to carry water up to the church the next day. There was too much to do to be here, sweating and puffing and hurting.

"Come on, Elroy!" he said again.

He knew Elroy couldn't hear him by now, but it was a kind of prayer, a way of distracting himself from the idea that he might actually be dying.

He tried to focus on other thoughts: the mountain laurel along the rocky trail they were following; the cold stream where they bathed and fished for trout; the sounds of night on the side of the mountain.

Still, it came back to throbbing pain. His right leg now felt swollen and misshapen, as if he had elephantiasis. The pain radiated out in waves with each pump of his heart, which seemed to be laboring with more difficulty on each beat. When he closed his eyes, he was beginning to see vivid colors.

"This is not good . . ." he said aloud. "The King got me, and I wish it'd been a damn copperhead!"

He couldn't wait for help. He had to get off the mountain. He forced himself out of the sleeping bag and was shocked at the sight of his own swollen leg. The passing thought occurred to him that if he hadn't been wearing shorts, the swelling would have ripped his jeans off. Even so, he began stumbling down the mountain trail, one shoe on, one shoe off.

"Elroy!" he yelled. "I gotta get some help! Elroy!"

He ambled forward, half falling, half jogging, almost in a dream state of madness, occasionally using a tree trunk or a large rock to help himself back up. At times he wasn't sure whether his eyes were open or closed. Sweat was dripping off his forehead in spite of the summer's evening coolness.

When he could go no further, he allowed himself to fall onto a limestone outcropping that was arranged like a tilted bench near the trail. He heaved air in and out, trying to give oxygen to his starved system.

He couldn't be far from the parkway now. They had seen on their map that they were within a mile or so before the accident happened. In fact, if a car came along he would probably be able to see the headlights from here. He began scanning the night for signs of light. At first, his eyes played tricks on him, and a lone lightning bug became a box truck driving toward him, or a star peeking between the branches of a tree became a distant car approaching. But then he saw something lighter and bigger, close by in fact.

It was body. With a tan jacket.

"Elroy!"

Colson stumbled forward again and drew up just short of his friend's motionless body. Elroy's face was swollen, and his arms and legs had several visible puncture marks on them. Beyond Elroy's body was a small swale in the rocks and Colson could see something writhing or moving, indistinct but unmistakably not rock. He fumbled through his shirt pockets and found a book of matches, trying several times before succeeding in striking one.

"Oh, Elroy . . ." he said slowly. Beyond his friend's contorted body was a mass of small copperheads, moving in and around each other like a living ball. Each one was barely eight inches long. "You'd a been better off with The King . . ."

Behind him, flashlights were bobbing closer and closer. A ranger was suddenly beside him.

"You okay, son?" he asked. "What happened?"

Suddenly, thoughts began to slow down in Colson's head. He would be married in a month; he would meet his brother; he would (maybe) go to church tomorrow.

But Elroy . . .

"Snake bit," Colson said.

The deputy put Colson's arm over his shoulder and led him away.

If God Gave Me Wings

Gwendolyn Thompson Poole

(Third place fiction, Blue Ridge Writers Chapter contest, VWC, 2016)

"You're such a scaredy-cat, Addie," Rose said as she squatted and poked a stick at something in the dirt.

"Am not!" Addie snapped and stood up.

"Nothin' but a dead bird. Can't hurt you. C'mon, I'll race you to de barn!" Rose called as she dropped the stick and headed across the yard. She ducked under the clothes drying on the line and heard Bessie holler after her. In the distance, she heard the chant of the men and women in the field. It was a familiar tune that gave her a sense of belonging. Growing up a slave on Virginia soil was all Rose knew. She was born on this plantation and was fortunate not to have been sold away from her mama and papa. Her smooth, dark skin glistened with perspiration as her long legs stretched to carry her to the barn. Rose's bare feet pounded the earth as her little, brown sack dress danced around her slight, ten-year-old frame. Addie followed.

It was a warm afternoon as the sun began to fade behind the mountains, allowing the last of its rays to linger on the young tobacco stalks and wheat that stood proudly in the still, warm air. The valley was rich in agriculture and called the breadbasket of the state. Almost anything could grow here. The vast acres of rich, fertile soil were a tapestry of design laid carefully by the instructions of the planters. The rolling hills and pastures were dotted with livestock grazing in the fields. This land was beautiful. It seems as if God pushed up the Allegheny Mountains on the west and the Blue Ridge on the east and then smiled down on this hollowed out place, this valley known as Shenandoah.

The big farmhouses and plantations were prominent throughout the valley, and many of the wealthy families depended heavily on the profits of slave labor. The slaves were forced to live in the quarters loosely scattered within a safe distance of the "big house." Everything in the Shenandoah Valley seemed to hold its breath, bracing for the hot summer and what it would bring.

It was late spring in 1864, the U.S. Civil War was in full swing, and Virginia had been the site of a number of battles. However, only a few had been in the valley. Confederate general Thomas Jonathan "Stonewall" Jackson, just two years prior, had led his troops to defend the northern end of the valley. It was a small conflict with few casualties, but the effect was favorable for the southern forces. In 1863 General Robert E. Lee used a route along the Shenandoah Valley to push back Union general George B. McClellan's army that was threatening Richmond, the Confederate capital. News of the skirmishes to the north as well as the recent bloody campaign that erupted near Petersburg to the east had traveled to Lexington. Any news that had reached the slaves in Lexington came by way of snatches of conversations overheard from messages delivered to the masters.

Life in Lexington and the southernmost tip of the Shenandoah Valley remained relatively peaceful and undisturbed at the beginning of the war. However, there was the constant concern that, in time, this part of the valley would surely be hit. Since April 1861, when the war had begun, many of the men had gone off and joined the Confederate Army, which left the women, aged and infirmed men, and the children to run the farms. Some young, able-bodied slave men ran off to support the Union Army. Aside from keeping journals and account books for their farms, overseeing the operations in absence of their husbands, fathers, and brothers, the white women wrote and received letters from their men at war. They shared the news with others as they sat and sewed and assisted with household chores, celebrating the bravery of their menfolk, all the while wishing the war would end. The slave men and women moved quietly about as they listened to the reports, hoping to hear some word of one of their own.

The Virginia Military Institute, which was referred to as the West Point of the South, had prepared its cadets for battle even though they had seen none. The young men continued to study, train, and remain alert. The citizens of Lexington were proud of the VMI boys as they were seen about the town.

"Wait for me!" Addie called to Rose. Addie was the master's child, born to a slave woman, Tess, almost ten years ago. Because of her fair complexion, she worked in the "big house" with Mama Tess and other house servants and didn't have much time to spend outside as did Rose, who lived down in the slave quarters. Addie was often teased by the other slave children because of her hazel eyes and sandy-colored hair. They didn't like the fact that she was the only one of the slave children permitted to play on the front lawn of the "big house" with little Sarah Ann, daughter of the master and missus.

Rose panted hard and leaned against the horse barn as Addie approached. "I beat you," she said breathlessly.

"'Cause you had a head start," Addie responded as she sprawled in the grass shaded by the old barn. The sky was clear and Addie's gaze fell upon a single bird that lazily glided overhead. "What if God gave us wings so we could fly? Where would you go, Rose?"

"If God gave me wings, I'd fly all de way to freedom, wherever dat is, up Nof, I s'pose. Preacher say God din't make us to be no slaves. Say slavery is evil."

Addie rose up on her elbows and looked around. "You betta hush yo mouf else you gonna get us whupped fo' talking 'bout freedom," she whispered fiercely.

Rose peered around to look inside the barn, but no one was there, not even the horses or mules. Earlier she had seen Jacob preparing the horse and buggy for Master's trip and both the work mules were out in the field. She focused her attention again on Addie. "I know a secret," Rose whispered as she slumped in the grass beside her friend.

"What secret?" Addie asked.

"Promise not to tell?" Rose asked.

"Promise," Addie agreed.

"Well dis morning," Rose began, "Miz Hannah sent me 'long with Missy Caroline to Col Alto, so's I can tote some things back for her. I think Missy really like me 'cause she let me walk 'long 'side her an' she talk real nice to me, just like I's one of her friends."

"She's gon git you whupped fo' being uppity, dat's what she gon do!" Addie scolded emphatically.

"She only let me walk 'long 'side her if'n nobody coming. When we see one of dem cadets coming 'long de road, Missy hold her head up high as to ignore me and I falls in step behind her."

"So what's de big secret?" Addie prompted.

"When we got to Col Alto, Missy Caroline told me to wait just outside de back do. Have you ever been to Col Alto, Addie?"

"No, but I hear it sure is a pretty place," she answered as she leaned away from the path of a bumblebee.

"It got de prettiest flower gardens all 'round de whole house. After standing by de do a spell waiting fo Missy, I took a notion to walk over to smell some of de flowers. Well, I smelled a few here and a few dere and de next thing I knowed, I was far down in de middle of de flower garden when I thought I heerd somebody crying. So I peered through de rose bushes an saw a little sitting place with a swing, a bench, a little table, and some glasses of lemonade. An' dere was a man an' a woman sittin' in de swing. They din't see me, but de lady was de prettiest white woman I ever seen, far prettier dan Missy Caroline. She had long dark curls dat hung down from her bonnet an' rested on her shoulders. Dere was not even a blemish on her face an' even wit her crying, her blue eyes had a sparkle. An', Addie, whoever be caring for her dresses done a fine job! I think it was de blue of de dress dat made me notice her eyes. De dress an' her eyes, dey both de same color!"

"So tell me 'bout de secret. Was dey kissing?" Addie asked with enthusiasm.

"No, she was crying a little, you know, kinda soft like an' she was holding a fancy little handkerchief," Rose explained. "Den de man got up an' walked straight toward de bush an' my heart almost stopped. I thought he look right at me!"

"Why din't you run?"

"My feet wouldn't let me. Seem like dey was planted in de ground like two stalks of corn. I froze. He had a worried look on his face, de kinda look Ole Joe has when he know he be in trouble with Massa. Den he turned to de lady and say, 'I din't mean to make you cry.' An' she say, 'But, Charles, you

72

din't go to war in order to stay and oversee yo place!' Den he say, 'But I just have to do dis. Don't you understand, for me, for de South!' De lady dabbed at her eyes again and pouted. 'What 'bout for me, Charles, what 'bout for me? I surely can't marry you if'n you go off to war and be killed. For months and months, Mother has been planning everything, down to de smallest detail. Why it's going to be de grandest day in all of Rockbridge County! I hate all dis war business! It's ruining everything, even de most important day of my life! Why does dis stupid old war have to interfere wit our plans? Everyone thought it would be over no sooner that it started.' Den she walks over to him and say, 'Anyway, my gown is de prettiest thing you're ever laid eyes on. 'Course you won't git to see it 'til our wedding day. Our wedding day—doesn't dat just sound delightful, Charles? Doesn't it?' Mr. Charles looks away an' den de lady start to cry harder into her handkerchief an' he went an' put his arm 'round her."

Addie put her hand to her mouth to stifled a laugh as she watched Rose prance around and change her voice to imitate the white lady. Then she asked seriously, "What was dat Mr. Charles talking 'bout to upset de lady so?"

"He was talking 'bout going off to war, Addie. Say wit de country split up and de Nof fighting de Souf, he want to do his part, say he want to keep dem Yankees off dis Virginia soil, even if he have to die to do it. But listen to dis, Addie, he say dat if de Souf lose de war, den we all be free! Dere be no more slavery! Say if de Nof win, all de Niggers be set free an' dere be none to work de land or in de iron plants an' de Souf would lose everything!"

Addie jumped to her feet. "Now I know you betta hush up!" she whispered fiercely.

"But it be de troof, what I heerd! We better tell somebody," Rose exclaimed.

"You betta keep dat truth to yoself! If'n you get caught 'peatin' white folks' business, you asking fo' trouble in a mighty big way. C'mon, let's go back up to de yard."

They ran back up toward the yard and joined the other women who were taking down the laundry. They worked hard the rest of the day, snapping beans, shucking corn and mending and didn't have much to say to each other, or anyone for that matter. Then Rose whispered a single word to Addie, "Wings."

Celestial Immortality

Martha Jean Lancaster

Kindred souls believe they have been born of the same womb, separated at birth, but perhaps attached for life. This kind of connection was at the heart of the friendship between Callie, Pete, and Harry. The teenagers trusted the notion of immortal flesh and blood as they challenged and depended on each other. Their bond would be eternal, or so they had convinced themselves until the accident a year ago last summer.

Now in mid-August, they embarked on the last of their *twelve labors*. Their Hercules-inspired tasks had propelled them through 1969 and their senior year in high school. They had chosen one challenge for each month beginning the previous September. In two weeks, they would disperse to colleges that had selected them based on legacy status and not on their academic merit. For now, though, they were all in the school of *carpe diem*.

Today, the eighteen-year-olds steamed like red-hot crabs in the sweltering rays that roasted the '64 VW van. The boxy vehicle had aged one-hundred-thousand miles in two years of cross-country and short trips during summer and spring breaks.

Pete piloted the vehicle like a wayward sea captain. He only needed a curved, hand-carved tobacco pipe to enhance his weathered appearance. He crushed his hat brim down over his sweaty forehead. He had not groomed his scruffy beard at all during the two months since they graduated in early June.

While Pete was the captain, Callie and Harry posed as the drunken crew besotted by the salt air. Callie clung tight to the inside back door handle, her honey-brown hair blowing from windows stuck in the open position. Although Harry's bulk anchored him firmly in the front passenger seat, he still grasped the dashboard to keep from being tossed around.

Pete maneuvered the crusty van over the rough access road between the sand-sprayed dunes. The van's metal exterior was as dark green as ocean muddled under a cloudy sky. Dents scattered the sides of the vehicle like conical bubbles on the surface of a riptide.

Wrapping the full length of his arms around the steering wheel, Pete struggled to hold the van steady. Entering the beach, they followed a smoother, southerly path on sand that was packed hard by incoming tides. Driving the beach was much slower than if they had flown down the two-lane paved Route 12 highway that stretched the length of Hatteras Island. The travelers cruised as far as they could on a half-tank of thirty-five-cents-a-gallon Chevron gasoline. They saved half a tank to make their way back north over the Oregon Inlet Bridge the next day.

Pete eased to a slow docking about three miles south near Pea Island Refuge. He finally pulled the van to a stop where the tide was as low as the last froth of cucumber-melon bubble bath draining from a claw-foot tub. The retreating water left behind scurrying sand crabs, half-sunken fragments of conch shells, and sputtering sea bass on the damp, putty-colored shoreline.

"Hey, Callie, did you finish writing out our list of adventures from this past year?" Harry yelled. His voice carried over the bellow of the ocean that replaced the rumble of the now-quiet four-horsepower engine.

"Heck yes, finished it by the time we saw the Outer Banks sign," Callie answered.

"When we drain the last drops of that cheap tequila tonight, we'll roll up the list, cap it in the empty bottle, and toss our memories into the world of Neptune," Harry laughed, "And we'll send the worm with it."

They parked parallel to the ocean near the high tide line. Harry hoisted down the kayak and paddles strapped precariously on top of the van. Like the god of the sea, he was the muscle of the trio, well-toned from years as high school quarterback, but thankfully lacking Neptune's legendary temper.

Harry and Pete twisted long tent poles deep into the sand to anchor a tarp. They tied off the weathered canvas to the luggage rack to create a semblance of shade. Meanwhile, Callie hand-scooped a channel in the sand down to the layer packed like brown sugar. The guys unloaded the heavy cooler

76

of iced-down beer and bait and settled it in the shaded trough.

They unloaded their food rations of sodium-chloride carbs that included restaurant-style tortilla chips and salt-laden Fritos. Their vegetables were blended in a sixteen-ounce jar of extra-hot salsa. There would be no mild condiments for these motley mariners. There were no vitamin-C laden fruits to prevent scurvy on this twenty-four-hour voyage.

Harry and Pete carried two beach chairs and fishing tackle out to the surf's foamy edge. They cast their lines far out into the water and aimed for bubbled areas on the surface that indicated riptides carrying larger fish. The guys flopped down into the chairs, opened cans of Schlitz, and splayed their hairy legs out in the way that real men relax. They planned to snag dinner with eight-inch hooks hidden in cuts of scrap fish. They would toss their catch into a water-filled bucket to ponder their imminent gutting.

While they waited for nibbles, the guys scanned for fishing and shrimping boats that appeared randomly midway between the farthest waves and the ocean's horizon. They had their backs toward the hot cadmium-yellow sun. It resembled a large full moon when it was closest in the sky and had not quite started to descend to the earth's western edge.

While Pete and Harry fished, Callie wandered through the sea oats on the dunes. Small sharp sandspurs spiked the soles of her bare feet as she gathered driftwood for the bonfire. After she returned with an armful of dry wood, she spread out a thread-raveled quilt and donned large, white-rimmed sunglasses. She did not have any creamy 75-SPF sunscreen, as this was the era of using baby oil and iodine to sooth blistery tans.

Soaking up the sun, she flipped through issues of *Cosmopolitan* and sucked crushed ice Margaritas through the straw in her giant 7-Eleven Slurpee cup.

Lurking gulls swooped around waiting for Callie to toss pistachio shells in the sand. As though these birds were human and knew "what men want," she read the Cosmo quiz out loud and announced the multiple-choice answers to the attentive flock.

She could not hear what the guys talked about over the

din of the ocean, but she knew it must be akin to macho antics. She guessed it was a debate of who was the best fisherman or football player? Or even who was the most popular Don Juan in their school? Callie dozed off as the sun turned into a gloaming of sharp rays.

As the sunset began to color the sky, the guys started the cooking fire. When the flames tapered down to coals as red as Mars, Harry fried the fresh Croakers in a cast-iron skillet. Dinner was solemn and communal. The trinity of sun, sand, and sea saturated the three friends. They turned their beach chairs to watch the massive orb disappear behind the dunes. Scattered dark clouds moved over the Pamlico Sound on the west side of the finger strip of Hatteras.

After dinner, they splashed and body surfed as they skinny-dipped in the water cooled by the night. The three settled in to reminisce as they gathered around the fire to dry off. Their favorite memory was about Sister Bettina's kindergarten class at Saint Benedict Catholic School. They laughed as they remembered Harry as the squat bulky kid on the playground. He was the leader in kickball and protector of the littlest kids in the sandbox.

Pete was the golden child, teacher's pet, and the trickster Pan. They called him Panama Pete because of his favorite hat, a gift from his archeologist grandfather. This hat was his constant accessory after school and on weekends, when he would shed his schoolboy uniform of white shirt with the green-and-white, school-color tie.

Callie was a child of the water when she was young. She learned to swim at the Country Club of Virginia almost from the day she learned to walk. Callie was the quiet, pensive, and more academic one in their group of friends.

Their schoolmate Casey was always the pretty one— even in grammar school. Her skin was the light olive tone of her heritage. Her smile was perfect, even as baby teeth disappeared and permanent teeth took their places in a straight line. Her eyes were like the aged brown iron gall ink used by the Old Masters. Later, she was the most beautiful girl in their high school. With the vanity of the Greek queen Cassiopeia, Casey knew she was more beautiful than sea nymphs.

When Callie and Casey went to St. Gertrude's High School, the boys advanced to Benedictine College Prep. This was when a fifth friend joined their alliance. Zeke's family had just moved to Richmond, where he enrolled at Benedictine.

During those years in high school together, they would gather on Friday nights to wait in line under *Tantilla Garden*'s lighted marquee that rose like a jeweled tiara on Broad Street. In the second floor ballroom, they danced to the Escorts "Shake a Tail Feather" and the beach-and-soul music of Ron Moody and the Centaurs. They were "cooled by nature's breezes" when the roof rolled open to the stars. Their favorite occasion at *Tantilla* was a psychedelic dance party with its amazing light show. And of course, they brown-bagged liquor even though they were all underage. But no one asked for IDs in the late '60s.

On sultry summer evenings, they would sneak onto properties with *No Trespassing* signs like the Benedictine Abbey on River Road. Other nights when there was full moon, they would walk from Monument Avenue over to Cary Street and wander through the historic Agecroft Hall gardens, down to the railroad tracks, the Kanawha Canal, and the James River.

Their lives had always been connected to surging waters and the circling sky. Tonight on the beach they watched the waxing crescent moon appear just after the sun had set. Pete wandered off to gather more wood. With the fire refreshed, the flames ascended high above their heads. Pete, Harry, and Callie searched for shooting stars and for their patron constellations visible in the celestial sky.

Callie wondered if their future was concealed in the stars illuminating a sky painted a blue-black azure color. Although she and her friends were Catholic and should believe in the saints, they each had chosen a constellation that reflected their identity and dispensed inspiration.

Harry spotted the constellation Hercules, still visible in August. The stars of his right leg were lifted as if in dance. According to legend, his outstretched hand held the earth and the sky. Three of the *twelve labors* that the hero had defeated were the nearby constellations of Leo, Hydra, and Cancer.

Pete had a fascination with stars that existed in the

Milky Way. He claimed the Cruz, the Southern Cross, for his own patron. The constellation matched Pete's wandering ways and his navigator's instinct for finding the exact same spot on the beach the past two years of their pilgrimages here.

Harry and Pete had chosen Callisto for Callie's constellation. She forever circled the North Star and never touched the horizon. Callie thought of herself as virtuous like the Greek nymph who had vowed to remain a virgin.

Callie turned to gaze up at Cassiopeia, who appeared to be suffering, hanging upside down as punishment for her haughty vanity. Her sister stars were Alpha, Beta, Epsilon, Eta, Theta, and Mu. Cassiopeia was chained to her starry throne just as their friend Casey was now restrained in a wheelchair.

The bonfire raged with the flaming memories of a year ago when the group lost two of their original clan. Before that reckless accident, they thought of themselves as indestructible. Harry was driving the car when it crashed. As a result of the accident, Casey was paralyzed. Zeke had pulled her from the car before smoke and gas fumes annihilated him. The pain and sorrow of his heroism was immutable.

They had always thought Zeke would survive them all. He was their peacekeeper. He settled their adolescent disagreements. But, he was also an incessant flirt and an obsessive drinker. In high school, he was king of the tequila shots. Despite the fact that he was nonchalant toward her, Callie knew he had deeply loved her even if they had never gone all the way. Zeke must have been on all of their minds, when Harry spoke up first.

"So what's all this crap that only the good die young? Zeke wasn't perfect," Harry announced.

"That's bull. He was close to perfect. The girls all loved him. He was our leader, our Zeus," Pete said.

"Remember when he pulled that Greek mafia stunt. We pretended to abduct him from Willow Lawn shopping center? We piled into his father's black Lincoln Town Car. The windows were tinted so dark you couldn't see inside," Harry remembered.

"Zeke had all of us dress like Al Capone gangsters, black overcoats, fat cigars, and Fedora brims pulled down over our eyes. What a blast!" Pete said.

The guys guffawed and slapped high-fives sloshing beer suds all over Callie. "Hey, enough. Stop that!" she demanded.

"Thank God, our parents got us off of that rap," Harry said.

Turning to Pete, Callie said, "Mr. Peter Pan, now *you* are the merry prankster. Remember the night you were whipping doughnuts in that hay field? There were eight of us jammed in your Bimmer. We were so blitzed," she said. "I was scared to death when you raised your hands up over the steering wheel and said, 'Callie, you drive.'"

Tired of the ribbing aimed at him, Pete changed the subject back.

"So what about reincarnation? You think Zeke is that big sand crab over there, popping out of his hole to chase all those smaller females?" Pete asked.

"What? Are you a Buddhist now? Reincarnation?" Harry asked.

"I truly believe Zeke is a celestial soul or the brightest planet Jupiter," Callie said. "Or maybe he's in a constellation of the ancient Greeks. That was his reward."

"Or his punishment," Harry muttered.

"Or maybe it was just his time? Fatal fate strikes a final blow," Pete was usually not so serious as this.

"Whatever, it really sucks," Harry whispered. "It was all my fault."

The repetitive crash of the incoming tide drowned out Harry's sobs. The only visible evidence of immense sorrow was his head burrowed in his shaking arms.

In the early morning hours when time does not move, they rolled up their list of escapades that Callie had written in her flowing script. Harry pushed the paper tube into the empty tequila bottle and heaved it far out into the waves. They spread out sleeping bags around the crackling embers of the fire pit. The smoke carried their haunted dreams to the stars.

When the white-hot center of the sun began to rise at the edge of ocean, Callie woke up and stretched. She noticed the tide had buried their van in sand up to the axels. Pete was still asleep, but she didn't see Harry.

She noticed footprints in the sand, headed just one-way toward the water that was starting to wash them away. The furrow of a dragged kayak ran beside the imprints. She scanned around their campsite from one end of the beach to the other and back toward the dunes. She shielded her eyes from the rising sun above the ocean stretching out without any sign of a vessel floating on the surface.

Harry was always the one who stoked the dying coals in the morning to start a pot of coffee brewing, but Callie saw the metal percolator tilted in the sand. She gasped in the salty air so deep into her lungs that she choked. She realized there wasn't any sign Harry had ever been here with them at the never-ending ocean. Was this loss what their twelfth and final *labor* was really meant to be?

On the Cusp

Gary D. Kessler

Charlie looked down at his half-filled backpack and then at what was scattered around him in his room. It was obvious that everything he wanted to take wasn't going to fit. How had he let himself accumulate so much here with the Wilsons that he wouldn't want to leave behind? Always before he'd been able to just pack and leave. Of course, he'd never stayed as long in a foster home before as he had with the Wilsons—Janet and Ed and Old Eddie. That was the problem. He'd stayed so long here that it would be extra painful when they came to move him on to another home, as they inevitably would. Always before he'd signaled when he wanted to go by taking off on his own and saying he had enough of that home when he was caught and then just moved on to another home.

Always when he'd gotten close to wanting to stay with a family forever, knowing this wasn't in the cards for him, he'd broken it off. It was easier when he did the rejection than it was to be rejected.

He'd built up to today—had planned that it would be this morning that he left. Ed almost ruined those plans by asking him at breakfast if he wanted to go fishing at Lake Sherando—that Ed was going to go and try out the boat they had reconditioned and would enjoy the company. If Charlie hadn't already decided that today was the day, he sure would have wanted to go fishing with Ed. He'd helped get that boat floating again. But he said no—that he had a "what did you do this summer?" essay to write for the startup of school.

Ed had given him a bear hug and said, "OK, fine. Next time. I'll leave some fish in the lake for us next time." That hadn't helped. If Charlie had started up bawling there, like he wanted to do, Ed would have known that something was up.

He surveyed the room again. He could take the Walkman he'd found, broken, and Ed had tinkered with until it worked again. But he couldn't take all the clothes Janet had bought him. But the sweater she'd knitted for him, letting him pick the colors of the yarn—he'd certainly take that. And there was no way that he could take the tomato plant on the windowsill Old Eddie had shown him how to plant, the one where the cherry tomatoes were about to ripen. And not the old guitar Old Eddie had restrung for him, although maybe he could try to carry that along. But the chessboard was out of the question. Old Eddie had carved all of the ebony pieces and half of the oak ones before he'd shown Charlie how to carve the rest. With Old Eddie's gnarled hands, that was quite an effort.

Well, maybe he would take a few pieces Old Eddie had carved and the better-crafted ones of his own—just for remembrance.

But maybe that wasn't a good idea. It wouldn't make having left or getting settled in the next home any easier.

"Charlie. Charlie, are you up there?" The voice of Janet from the kitchen. "Can you come down and get the trash out for me, please?"

"Coming," he answered. He moved the half-filled backpack off the bed and sort of pushed it under the bed frame. Not all the way. Not far enough that Old Eddie didn't see it when he came into the room looking for Charlie a few minutes later but missed him because Charlie had gone downstairs to put the trash out.

Old Eddie stood in the doorway for a long moment, looking at the backpack—and at the neatly folded clothes Charlie hadn't bothered to take off the bed. And at the separated chess pieces, a couple of them having fallen out of the backpack when it was stuffed under the bed. He took his cell phone out of his pocket and punched in a preprogrammed number.

Downstairs Charlie could smell the fragrance of freshly baked chocolate chip cookies before he hit the kitchen.

"After you put the trash out, maybe you could help me decide if these cookies came out right," Janet said as he entered the room. Always soft spoken, the tentative "all I want to do is please" voice in a pillowy body covered by a worn cotton shirtdress. The signature ruffled apron, perpetually drying her hands on the white, wrinkled material. "I got distracted by a phone call and I'm not sure I got all of the ingredients in. And maybe a glass of milk with them." She smiled shyly at him.

She knew she'd baked them right, but there was something bothering Charlie this morning. She could tell. She could tell at breakfast that he'd wanted to go fishing with Ed. But for some reason he didn't. Maybe it *was* that essay he said he had to write. He didn't do anything special over the summer; they'd just done family activities and he'd helped Ed caulk the boat he'd taken out today. Maybe it wasn't an exciting enough summer for Charlie for him to want to write about. But what they'd tried to do was give him stability—nothing extravagant; just the feeling of family. He'd been in and out of so many foster homes already. They'd thought he just needed some stability for a change.

"I'm making tacos for lunch," she said, when Charlie came back from the trash bin. "Hope that will be OK with you." She knew he loved tacos. Her instinct told her she needed to hold him close today.

"Yes, fine," Charlie said, his voice a bit distant when he sat at the table and reached for the glass of milk with one hand and a chocolate chip cookie with the other. He didn't want to look at her. He fought off the ache of it.

"Care if I join you?" Old Eddie said as he entered the room. He was carrying a length of leather.

"Oh, this?" he asked when Charlie gave him a quizzical look. "You said you'd like a belt like I made for myself. I thought that maybe this afternoon we can go out to my shop and I'll show you how you can tool a design in this. And we could make you a belt—together."

"Yes. Yes, I'd like that," Charlie said, hesitating a bit. In fact he *would* like that. A belt was something he could take. He could wear it. And tacos for lunch would be a good sendoff. He could leave later this afternoon as well as this morning. That wouldn't be a drastic change in his plans.

But, man, they weren't making this easy for him. He should have left as soon as school was out in June. He didn't know how much more of this he could take in life. Some of the other kids had found permanent homes. But they weren't mixed race like him. He'd been told it would be hard for him—being wholly neither this nor that, floating between two worlds. And he was too old now for a permanent replacement. Hadn't

85

they always told him that before, the social workers?—that he needed to get adopted young to have a real family. They sure had been right. It didn't seem like he could win for losing.

* * * *

They were about finished with belt when a blast of the horn of Ed's truck in the driveway pulled Charlie and Old Eddie to the doorway of Old Eddie's shop.

"I wonder if he caught anything," Charlie said.

"You go on and ask him," Old Eddie said. "All that's needed now is to get a buckle attached to this. We'll drill the holes when we can get it around you and see where they should be."

Old Eddie was relieved that he'd managed to stretch this project out. He could have done it in half the time. He had Charlie do more of it than he had intended so that they wouldn't be finished until Ed could get back.

"Caught any fish?" Charlie asked, as he approached the truck.

"I caught a cat," Ed answered, taking a small cage out of the passenger side of the pickup. "Must have gotten up into the undercarriage of the truck while I was fishing and gone to sleep. Didn't get more than fifty yards down the road out of Lake Sherando before it started yowling something awful. Here, want to see it? It's a he, I think."

Charlie leaned down and looked into the cage. The kitten, a Tuxedo cat, was plastered to the back of the cage, all big eyes and puffy tail. Frightened out of its mind, Charlie supposed. Scared and uncertain, just like Charlie had felt each time he was brought into a new foster home.

Charlie's voice went soft, and he murmured to the kitten in a low, calm voice. "It's OK, kitty, you're home now. Safe and home." He looked up at Ed with a question in his eyes.

"Yes, of course we'll keep it," Ed said. "You can name him. Right now, I bet it's starved and needs some water. Might could use a bit of affection and reassurance too. Maybe you can take care of that. Go into the house and Janet will fix it up with bowls and a bed in the kitchen—unless you'd prefer to have it bedding down in your room. And she'll find some food for it. I stopped at the store in Waynesboro and picked up a tray and some kitty litter. You can come out to the truck for that when you get kitty here settled."

Charlie took the cage, climbed the stairs to the front porch, and went in the house, calling Janet's name.

Ed and Old Eddie stood there, looking at each other, a bit of a shared smile on their faces. Old Eddie nodded his head slightly. Then he put the belt aside—he figured and hoped he could finish that later—and hobbled on his lame leg up onto the porch and "whoofed" into one of the rocking chairs. Pieces of wood and a whittling knife sat on the small table beside the rocker, and he instinctively reached for a chunk of wood and the knife and started to whittle. Whittling wood was his way of dealing with stress and happiness and concern—and just about any other emotion that worked at him.

Ed walked to the porch but stayed below it, a foot on one of the steps and his elbow resting on his knee, his eyes on Old Eddie but his ears tuned to the house. He was waiting for something. They both were waiting for something, barely being able to breathe the wait was so heavy.

Janet came out onto the porch, a slight smile on her lips and tears in her eyes. She sat in the rocking chair beside Old Eddie. "I think they've bonded already," she said.

Ed and his dad simultaneously letting out their breath was audible across the porch.

"Do you think—?" Ed started to say.

"I think he's the one. He's a keeper," Janet said, as she lifted the hem of her apron and rubbed it across her eyes.

"We're not talkin' about the cat now, are we?" asked Old Eddie, not looking at Janet, eyes only for the piece of wood he was whittling on.

"No, we're not talking about the cat," Janet answered. "But have we waited too long, Ed? We're both in our fifties now. By the time—"

"We can let the boy decide," Ed answered in a soft voice. "All we can do is hope, talk it over with him, and tell the lawyer to go ahead with the papers if he wants us—if he wants us as much as we want him." He looked over at Old Eddie. "What do you think about the age thing, Pop?"

"Why ask me?" Old Eddie huffed. "I've got twenty years on you both and I decided on him the minute he walked into the house, looking as scared and needy as that cat you just dragged in. You haven't noticed how we've been loading him down with stuff so he'd need a Mac truck to leave us the way the social workers said he left those before us—not shiny new toys from the store, but stuff we and he have had a hand in together? I figure the cat should pretty much do it—somethin' you can neither walk away with or, if you've had a life like Charlie has, somethin' you can't easily leave behind."

"Sure am glad I got your call this morning, Pop."

"Good story about the cat in the undercarriage," Old Eddie said, with a little chuckle. "He didn't even ask how you happened to have a cat cage in the truck. And I'm glad I saw that two-tone kitten in the window of the pet store down in Waynesboro the other day. Reminded me right off of Charlie. I even said, 'Well, hello, Charlie,' to it, and it looked at me like it understood—like we was family. Never saw a creature before that was begging for the right home like that one was—well, not since the expression on Charlie's face the day he came to us. I think we timed this just right—for all of us."

"I wouldn't wait, though," he added after a short pause, shifting gears, now all serious in voice and expression. "I'd talk to the boy today. Now." He went back to whittling a "whatever" as he watched the two calm and steel themselves and move into the house, Ed's arm around Janet's shoulder.

Old Eddie had already decided that he'd never tell Janet and Ed just how close the timing on this had been—on the cusp between losing and winning.

Tightrope Walker

Olivia Stowe

"What color are my eyes, Nick?" Emily suddenly blurted out. Her eyes weren't turned to Nick, sitting beside her on the small set of bleachers in the tent beside the Wabash River, though. They were plastered to the wire running overhead halfway between the ground and the curve of the tent ceiling, where a young woman was nervously and gingerly making her way across a tight rope. This wasn't a big, professional circus like had wintered here in Peru, Indiana, in the heyday of the town. This was the tail end of the third-week-in-July Peru Amateur Circus festival that celebrated the era of the big circus. The emphasis here was on the word "amateur."

The girl on the tightrope didn't look like she was going to make it across. She was an amateur at it, though, and had a strong-looking net under her, so the thrill of the danger just wasn't there. At least it wasn't there for most of those on the bleachers in the tent, although they were good-naturedly enveloping the tightrope walker with words of encouragement. The girl had been standing close to where Emily and Nick sat before she climbed the ladder, and Emily had seen the color of the girl's eyes, an unusual shade of hazel, like her own. She'd also seen the fear and a touch of desperation—a lack of confidence and self-esteem—in the young woman's eyes. And thus Emily had identified with the girl. Emily wouldn't have made it across the tightrope. Of this she was sure. She didn't think the young woman would be making it across either.

Nick hadn't been watching the tightrope act. His gaze had been roaming the bleachers, picking out girls who appealed to him. He wasn't looking at Emily.

"Huh, what? What'd you say?" he asked. He'd heard her say his name, but he still didn't look at her.

"I said, what are the color of my eyes?"

"Blue?" The question was obvious in his response. He still didn't look at her. Emily felt she had a right to be upset by that. Twenty minutes earlier, he'd been on top of her—inside her—in the backseat of his double cab Dodge Ram truck in a dark, remote row of the parking lot of the Miami County fairgrounds. He'd been all sweet talk and attention when they'd arrived at the carnival and had plied her with a chili dog and beer before luring her to his truck.

"My eyes are hazel, Nick. They're almost green. They always have been. They were hazel when you were on top of me in your truck and looking into my face."

"Whatever," he said, not anywhere close to being tuned in to her.

She stood in the stands and brushed off her skirt, giving him plenty of time to see that she wanted to leave. But he wasn't looking at her. He'd made eye contact with a redhead on the stands on the other side of the tightrope that the nervous girl was teetering on, not yet a third of the way across.

Jessica. Jessica Martin, Emily thought, recognizing the other young woman. Not that that was a challenge. Peru was a small enough town that everyone knew everyone else. Floozy, Emily thought. But then she bit her tongue. No one thought any less of Jessica in this town than they did of Emily. She knew she'd earned that reputation. It was, she now knew, why Nick had brought her to the last day of the circus carnival. And she'd delivered already.

She worked her way down from the bleachers. A few of the guys who helped guide her way through the seats having already had their turns touching her more intimately over the last couple of years since she'd graduated from high school in Peru and had just remained here. Nick was busy communicating in winks and lip licking with Jessica across the tent and didn't see Emily go.

When she got to the tent entrance, a gasp that floated over the bleachers caused her to turn and look. The girl on the tightrope—the scared-looking girl with the hazel eyes—had fallen into the net. She hadn't even made it halfway across the rope.

"It figures," Emily muttered and turned and walked out onto the lane that was lined with game booths and side shows under the uneven and flickering lights strung overhead on poles. The flickering light also figured, she thought. Here in the town that had been the first one in the world with electrified street lights, the light couldn't even remain steady until the end of the circus carnival. The town was slowly dying, and Emily was slowly dying right along with it—each and every time she fell off the tightrope.

* * * *

It wasn't a date. She wouldn't have come here with Nick on a date, so she didn't really have a kick that he was back there in the circus tent making goo-goo eyes with Jessica Martin. And he hadn't dragged her kicking and screaming to his truck. She'd always wondered what it would be like to be with Nick. It was telling that she went with him just for having gotten a chili dog and a beer—and, oh, yes, a cone of cotton candy and a little less than half of a funnel cake. But she'd gone with him too because that's what she did, what was expected from her in this town. The only times guys in this town gave her any attention was when they were sniffing around her, wanting something, but only wanting it in the short term. And Nick was a strapping young Swede—broad shouldered, blond, and good looking even if not all that bright. She didn't, at the moment, think she had much on him in the not-all-that-bright department, though.

But he was like so many other guys born and raised in Peru—content with farming or construction jobs until they could break away and go to a bigger city or, worse, content with staying what they were in Peru and growing old but never growing up. She didn't know what other kind of guy there was in Peru, but she'd tried all of these guys and she wanted the other guy. The problem was that she also wanted to be wanted—to be noticed and to be given attention and some credit for something other than her willingness to "put out"— which wasn't turning out all that well.

Emily had wanted to come to the amateur circus held every year here in Peru, the home also to the International Circus Hall of Fame because so many major circuses had wintered here, but she was making an effort to change her life. Guys had asked her to come with them, but they all were guys who would want what Nick got as part of the deal. Emily

91

hadn't thought she was coming here on a date. Her girlfriend, Amber, had suggested they come together, a simple girls' night out that had snowballed. Unknown to Emily that meant they'd hitch a ride with Amber's older brother, Nick. And, beyond that, Amber, who was still living with her parents, although she had a job, like Emily did, was using Emily as a blind. They both were room maids at the Cole Porter Motel that Emily lived behind in one of the cabins that had been the motel before the one was built in front. Amber's plan was to meet up at the carnival with the boyfriend, Tony, her parents didn't like. Within moments of arriving, Emily suddenly was here just with Nick.

Emily would have it out with Amber come Monday morning at the motel, but that didn't help her much tonight. Amber was a rat. Thinking of that made Emily smile, if only a bittersweet smile. It was Tony who was the rat—more of a ferret. Emily agreed with Amber's parents on Tony. Nick didn't, though. For some reason he and Tony were buds. They couldn't be more different—Nick blond and tanned, both hulking and a hunk, working under the sun in construction, and not all that bright. Tony was small and dark and like a ferret, but clever and scheming, and working as a garage mechanic. Greasy, but Amber was head over heels for him. Nick wouldn't squeal on them to his parents and he hadn't seemed to object to the chance to get Emily alone.

Emily had more than half a notion to tell Amber's parents, but she didn't have much ground to stand on—she'd willingly lain under their son in his truck while Amber and Tony were doing who knows what where? And Emily didn't think the Stinsons had much good to say about her either.

Emily heard her name being called and drifted over to one of the permanent open-sided sheds on the county fairgrounds, where a red-hot flame, leaping out of the maw of a metal oven, lit up an area that extended out into the midway. Two men, one younger and one older, were working inside the railing, stripped to the waist and putting on a glass-blowing demonstration. She hadn't recognized the voice, but as she drew to where people were standing around three sides of the shed watching the process, she recognized the muscular younger man, who had a glob of molten glass at the end of a four-foot-long-stemmed blowpipe and was working at forming the molten mixture into a vase. He'd blown it out into a bulb on a narrow stem and was spinning the pipe and working the shape with a paddle.

"Come on over here, little darlin'. I'll make something just for you."

His name was David. He had been one of Emily's last-year men. She hesitated, in no way in the mood to be reminded of men of her past, but those in the gathering around the shed had turned to her, smiling, and had parted for her to approach the railing.

"Hello, David," she said—forming the words tentatively as she approached.

"Do you like the color orange?" he asked, giving her a smile and extending the long metal pipe toward her.

"Not that much," she admitted.

"How about trimmed in green, like your eyes?"

He'd remembered the color of her eyes. Tonight, a guy was half way home with her just to be that attentive to her.

David turned and gestured to the other man, who pulled a long metal spike out of the furnace. The molten glass glob at the end of this was an emerald green. He extended it to hover over the orange vase form on the end of David's tube, dripping small globs of green on the orange, which David was swirling around on the orange with his paddle, making a lace effect on the surface of the forming vase. A good-sized glob dropped onto the ground. The crowd let out an "Aww" sound at seeing that and then an even louder "Aww" sound as, David, too much of his attention going to Emily, let the orange vase collapse into itself.

"Oh," Emily said. Her eyes went to the circular glob that had dropped to the ground in a raised circular pattern.

"Too bad," David said. But as he saw where Emily was looking, he smiled, grabbed a long, sharp spike from the maw of the oven, and spiked the emerald-green glob, boring a hole near the rim of it before the glass had hardened.

"But maybe you like a green pendant then," he said.

"Yes, I love emerald green," she said and smiled, as he raised the glob of glass.

"Then you must have it, little darlin'," he said. "You can touch it. It's just warm now. Here, I have a strip of leather we can use to make a necklace out of it."

She took it in her hand. The people around were watching them, but she didn't see them. All she saw was a lovely piece of glass—and, more important, a gift. A freely given gift. She'd had damn few free gifts given to her in her lifetime. She watched, almost in tears, as David wove the leather strip through the hole in the glass slug, knotted it, and lifted it to put over her head.

He brought his lips close to her ear and murmured to her as he pulled the necklace over her head. The smile froze on her face. She was back to where there were no freely given gifts. He wanted something for the "gift." She didn't lose her smile and, falling off that tightrope yet again, wanting the necklace, she nodded her assent to David. But she pulled away from the railing and slipped out of the gathering around the shed and into the dimmer lighting of the carnival midway. Not now, not this moment. She wasn't sure if the net would hold if she fell again so quickly.

Her first instinct was to go back to the tent—and Nick—but she saw that the crowd was coming out of the tent before she got there, and there was Nick, with Jessica clinging to his arm, Nick's eyes only for Jessica. Emily turned in the other direction and walked along the line of game booths on the midway. She saw Amber and Tony at a shooting gallery and moved toward them, but they weren't there when she got to the booth. She stood there, confused and not knowing where to turn to next, her gaze going to the line of beat-up tin ducks slowly parading across the back of the shooting range and then up to the shelf over them where the stuffed animal prizes were lounging.

"Which one would you pick?"

Emily turned her head toward the voice. He was connected with the carnival part of the circus setup, she thought. It wasn't just that he was wearing a red suit, with sparkly sequins on it, which marked him as part of the show, but also because he'd been standing on a box at the entrance of the grounds when Amber, Nick, and she had come in and had been directing people to the various parts of the carnival. He had caught her eye then and had smiled to her.

So, he must be what they call a barker, Emily thought. He was a good-looking guy—normal looking, but well put together and he had a nice, confident smile. She had that old feeling of pulling herself up on a tightrope platform again. She just couldn't help herself from making the effort again. She fingered the glass slug at her neck. It was still warm. She blushed at the memory of the words David had used to proposition her. If only it was a guy with some sense of staying power—one who would pay attention to her for more than sex. She hadn't left David the previous year; he'd moved on from her.

"Excuse me?" she said.

"I asked which one you would pick—which of those stuffed animals, if you won a shooting prize. By the way, did anyone tell you you had a nice smile, and the prettiest green eyes—just like that stone around your neck?"

"Hazel."

It was his turn to say, "Excuse me?"

"My eyes. They are hazel." She said it haltingly, though, it somehow not being as important a point with this guy as it was with Nick—like maybe something more than eye color was behind her reaction.

"But they look almost green from here—like that stone."

"It's glass, not stone." But then he was looking confused, and she didn't want him to think she was making fun of him. "The tiger. I think I'd pick the tiger. Are you going to win it for me?" She gave him a shy smile.

"I think you can win it for yourself. There's a secret to this. Come on up to the rail. I'll stake you a couple of shots. I think you'll prize the tiger more if you win it yourself."

She took another look at him. No one had shown such confidence in her before. And, yeah, she should be able to win her own prizes. She should stop depending on guys who weren't dependable and wanted something for whatever they gave her.

"My name is Ryan, by the way," he said as he guided her to the rail and gestured for a rifle to be given to them. He stood there, holding the rifle and looking at her expectantly.

"Uh, I'm Emily," she said, finally getting that he wanted a name for a name. Smiling, he showed her how to hold the rifle and murmured in her ear—so much different from what David, the glassblower, had whispered to her. Ryan was telling her how she could triumph, not trying to get something out of her.

"Don't aim at it. Aim just a bit ahead of it. And wait for the next one to come to you. Don't move back to it."

After the gallery attendant had taken the stuffed tiger down from the shelf and handed it to her, Emily turned her head to thank Ryan for his help—and for the confidence he'd shown in her ability to do it herself—but he was gone. That didn't keep her from having the feeling that she'd stood at the edge of the tightrope and, for the first time, contemplated taking that first step without the fear of falling.

* * * *

"Can I have a lovely volunteer from the audience to be my assistant for the next trick? You, perhaps. The young woman with the green eyes." He was smiling at her impishly.

Hazel, Emily immediately thought, but she blushed as Ryan gestured to her from the small raised platform and those standing around in the magician's tent turned to look at her. She hated being the center of attention. So why, when Ryan extended his hand toward her, did she smile, close her hand around the glass slug at her neck, and allow him to take her up onto the stage?

For that matter, why, when she was passing by the open flap to the magician's tent and hearing a familiar voice, did she look in, and, seeing Ryan in his red sequined suit performing on the stage, did she enter? And why was the image rising in her mind of standing on a platform, looking out onto the high wire, and not being afraid to take that first step?

"Just go with the act," Ryan whispered to her as she was handed up to the stage. "It's just an illusion, but it's entertainment. You can help maintain the fantasy, can't you?"

He was trusting her. He needed to entertain these people and he was trusting her to go with the illusion. He needed her. No man had given her that much regard before. She gave him a smile. At this point she would have given him anything he wanted.

"Here, I'll hold your tiger for you for the moment," he said loud enough for all in the tent to hear. "Now you promise he won't maul me, will you?" Titters floated through the tent. The audience was with him.

"No, he won't bite you," she answered in a serious voice, which increased the laughter. She blushed. They'd thought she was just playing along with him, when she was so taken with him that she couldn't think straight.

"Pose nicely beside this box," he whispered. "Show them how lovely you are. Make them look at you rather than anywhere else on the set."

Emily leaned against the side of the black box in a pose she imagined a magician's assistant would take. She was fully into the illusion now.

Ryan explained how Emily would go into the box and disappear. He gave her a reassuring look as he put her into the box. He did his hocus pocus routine, threw open the box, and, sure enough, Emily wasn't there. She had almost laughed at how simple it was when a stagehand, lifting a finger to his mouth, pulled her back into the intricate set that looked like a flat wall from in front but wasn't. He hustled her out of the back of the tent and around to the front and inserted her into the crowd while Ryan was distracting the audience, which, good-naturedly cooperating, was ooing and ahing over the elaborately demonstrated empty box.

With a flourish Ryan looked out into the crowd, took up the stuffed tiger, and called out to the audience, "You, beautiful lady with the green eyes, would you like your tiger back? I think he misses you."

Those around where Emily was standing turned to her and ooed and ahhed in amazement at her sudden appearance amongst them, whether genuine or feigned to help hold the magic, it didn't matter. Emily was beaming. It was all magic to her. The whole night seemed magical to her now. In her mind, she was taking that first step out onto the tightrope—and she wasn't falling.

As the audience drifted out of the tent, Ryan came down off the stage to Emily and handed her the tiger.

"Thank you. You were terrific."

"No, *you* were terrific," she said, mesmerized by him.

"That was my last show for the night, and the carnival is shutting down. Do you have someone to take you home?"

She couldn't speak; she just gestured that she didn't— realizing only now that she, in fact, didn't have anyone to take her home—with her head.

"Have you ever ridden on the back of a motorcycle?"

It might as well be a magic carpet, she thought. He'd take her home, back to her cabin behind the motel. She'd let him come in, and they'd . . . no, she'd just fall off the tightrope again. She'd just do what she'd always done, and he'd be just like the others. But maybe not. Maybe this would be different. Maybe she could trust him.

"But perhaps you don't want me to take you home on my motorcycle."

"No, that would be fine. That would be terrific," she said, trying to give him a smile, which was so much harder now than it had been just a few minutes earlier when everything was magical.

It wasn't a long ride, but long enough for her to play out what would happen in the cabin in her mind—where she always wound up—taking that first step across the tightrope and falling into the net below.

But when they arrived at her cabin and she hopped off the back of the motorcycle, Ryan remained on it. "Thank you for playing along so well back there for the magic act. You were great. And you do have the loveliest green eyes, even if they really are hazel."

And then he putted off on his motorcycle, gearing up and picking up speed only when he was well away from where she was standing, confused, relieved—but, yes, a little disappointed.

"Tiger," she exclaimed, realizing only then that Ryan had ridden off with her stuffed tiger in his saddlebag. She trudged into her cabin, feeling the loss of her stuffed tiger, but with some part of her realizing that it wasn't really the tiger she felt the loss of. For just a brief time there, at the carnival, she had been alive and in a magical world.

But now she was in Peru, Indiana, again, entering her small cabin behind the motel where she worked as a room maid. Her dream man in the red sequined suit would be evaporating tomorrow with the close of the circus carnival. And any day now, the glassblower David would be showing up to claim payment for a dollop of green glass he'd speared off the ground. And once more she'd be falling off the tightrope.

* * * *

"Oh, I don't know if I'm up for ice cream today."

"That's OK, I don't know what Tony will want to do anyway," Amber answered, stowing the sweeper away in its closet in the storeroom behind the motel lobby while Emily stacked unused folded sheets on another shelf. Their day was done cleaning the motel rooms, and they had been discussing what they'd do with the rest of the day. Amber had suggested going to Malt Town, which had recently reopened on South Broadway under new ownership.

Emily bristled, but she turned away so that Amber wouldn't see it. She was still ticked at Amber for ditching her at the carnival the previous Saturday night and leaving her at the mercy of Amber's brother, Nick. But it wasn't like Emily had a lot of girlfriends and could afford to lose her friendship with Amber. Still being upset, though, had been the only reason she turned down a trip to the ice cream parlor after work. She, in fact, was dying for a vanilla shake.

"So, where will you and Tony go then?" she asked.

"He wants to drive over to Mexico and take a look at a Dodge Super Bee he's thinking of buying and flipping to resell." Mexico wouldn't be as far a drive as those not from

99

Indiana might think. Those choosing town names for Indiana's Miami County had been long-distance thinkers, having included Peru, Warsaw, Kokomo, and Mexico on the county map.

After watching Tony drive up in his pickup and then roaring off with Amber in a cloud of exhaust fumes, Emily felt safe enough to walk over to South Broadway and to the newly reopened Malt Town herself. She did a double take when she entered and saw who was standing behind the counter.

"Ryan," she exclaimed. She recognized him by his smile even without the red sequined carnival barker's suit.

"In the flesh. I was hoping you'd come in here sooner rather than later. Tigger the tiger has been growling for you." He pulled Emily's stuffed tiger prize out from underneath the counter and she happily took it from him and hugged it. She had tried to pretend she hadn't minded the loss of the prize she'd won herself, but she'd just been fooling herself.

"You're here. I thought you traveled with the circus carnival."

"I did travel with it, but this was its last stop for the summer. My choice was to go home to Fort Wayne or to find something to do here until you came to pick up Tigger. Besides, I think any town with a beautiful woman with green eyes in it is someplace I'd like to hang around for a while."

Emily blushed, resisting to point out again that her eyes were hazel. But that didn't matter anymore to her. They were close enough to green, and Ryan was close enough to who she wanted to see on the platform at the other end of that tightrope, a man who could give her courage and confidence to step out over the void and not fall. But was he just like all of the other guys in this town—content with being nowhere and going nowhere other than flying off to a bigger city at the first chance to do so?

"How about a free vanilla shake to celebrate our opening—you look like a vanilla shake girl to me—and then I'll close up and we can take Tigger for another spin on my motorcycle."

"Giving away free shakes and closing the store in the middle of the day?" she asked. "Won't you get fired as quick as you got this job?"

"I don't think so. I own the store. I figure Peru is a good place to put down roots."

Well, well, well, Emily thought. "Yes, I'd love to take Tigger for a ride on your cycle," she said, taking a step out onto that tightrope, knowing now that she could do it, that she wouldn't fall into the net.

POETRY

Locus

Erin Newton Wells

The blade in the weeds beside a post
is hatchet flat but turned so it meets
earth head on. A hoe. Its dark iron
is alligator rough.

The shaft is eaten off by burial in dirt
a stump still wedged in a rusted slot
and no one to mend it or chop
hard ground in rows.

No one plants cotton now. The field
is sown in sorghum and tilled by
other means than back and hand.
A bleached sky bears down.

Mayhaw narrows the road and birds
still scrabble for the August cicadas.
The town sign is written Coton
the t plowed under.

A stand sells the local jam and jelly
and a shelf of mottled tomatoes.
A sheet of tin gives scant shade
to the one bare bench.

A few arrowheads are priced for sale
but the one hoe remains unmarked.
Flies mumble over cantaloupe
that no one attends.

A house sits well back under catalpa
with its useless beans. No one sings
in fields to make time pass in hard
chops of a forged blade.

A Fish

Erin Newton Wells

Along one line of finely pebbled shore
where forest finishes an edge she never

sees whatever lies beneath umber water
a glacier hollowed into chasms. A summer

sky smooths a nameless blue on water
and blurs heads of mountain upside down

upon its gloss. The birch repeat in streaks
of white. The spruce repeat in shadows

of a deeper blue. A forest that she leaves
behind is turned around on finely pebbled

shore. The sky becomes a place to walk.
A solitary cloud assumes its very center

and glides on glass above the blurring
mountain heads above the sheen of birch

and spruce. And she might go where
nothing mars a surface of a summer sky

on umber water except a silver pucker
on one cloud. It does not draw the water.

It does not pull it down in the chasms
that a glacier hollowed. Whatever moves

beneath the nameless blue gives another
pucker. And she might step from ring

to ring across the unseen water and walk
from kiss to kiss across a summer sky.

The Stranger

Susan M. Lanterman

He sulks behind impenetrable walls
Finding comfort in the shadows
He reclines in the darkness
Resisting the light of day
His innards are coiled
Aching from abuse

Hearing movement
He rises from his slumber
He slithers around the periphery of the room
Eying the unsuspecting
Beguiling the silent ones with his stare
He looms over them
Forcing his presence upon them
Pinning them in

Seeking escape, they feign politeness
His tongue flickers with disdain
He strikes with a piercing laugh
A captivating smile—thin and taut
He hovers and cajoles
And pours and pours and pours
Until he has seeped into their heads
Unraveled their tongues

The poison courses through his veins
Repulsed by the frivolous talk
He spews a rancid remark
An unintelligible blunder, an overt attack
All eyes fly to his shame
He wipes the corner of his mouth
An exaggerated motion
His hand fends off remaining stares
He casts the lot of us aside
Retreats to his lair

I sleep with a stranger
He rages and rages and rages
And falls like a thundering tree
Roots upended, crushing everything beneath
The silence is cavernous
Then night becomes day
The creature is subdued
Withdrawn into his fragile shell
The appearance of which
I once loved

Poor Man's Rain

David Black

(First place poetry, *Skyline* Summer contest, 2016)

The first cutting done, growth began to wane
as drought set in. The old man walked dry ground
each day praying hard for the poor man's rain.

He needed sunny days to grow the grain,
feed the pastureland, but wanted the sound
of thunder, an evening of welcome rain.

He'd pause from his work and stare at the vane
atop the barn, check the skies all around
for darkening clouds that might bring soaking rain.

An old broken man, walking with a cane
when he wasn't in the fields, but tight-bound
to this land by birth, needing some poor man's rain—

that was his dad's phrase, holding all the pain
of one whose days of work were hard and brown,
blessed if night brought an inch of saving rain.

That's the way it is above the earth, down
to your last dime and on your knees in vain,
a poor man headed toward that final mound,
whose dust will be settled by poor man's rain.

Live Birds, Dead Birds

David Black

(Honorable mention, Robert S. Sergeant Memorial Award,
Poetry Society of Virginia, 2016)

There are those who say our mountains,
if wind turbines were planted there,
would become killing grounds of swallows and
       hawks—

those high silvery blades would be
cruel silent slayers of fragile flying things.
Which may be, though as I walk
our sixty-five acres I muse

that I have never found the body
of a bird nor feathers beneath a tree.

How it is that sparrows, woodpeckers, and owls
can skim around a giant sycamore,
aviate a hundred thousand limbs and remain intact,
I don't know, but this morning

I found a dead titmouse on my back porch,
who perhaps in narcissistic admiration
flew into his own reflection

and broke his neck, or stupidly mistook
a sixty-foot-wide house for open air,

I thinking that as any bird neared a windmill
whose feet cleave to immobile earth,

it could flip a scornful wing
at those slow-moving blades
like a one-fingered salute.

Click-Bait Poetry

(First place poetry, Blue Ridge Writers Chapter contest, VWC, 2016)

Weeds: Those plants growing where we don't want
       them but
they still appreciate the sun as much as prized Iris.
Their flowers form
create seeds
attempt to see their progeny take root
maybe close by
not far away
though not caring if blown miles.
**#Dandelions Benefit From Climate Change and
     Pass on Good Genes**

Bluebirds: I look into the ragged box and see the stick
       nest where
four eggs huddled together earlier this week.
Then today I see
these hairy little pink marbles
they appreciate the sun
as much as I do
They nor the sun
know each other,
appreciation is not mutual.
Sunbeams are one-directional.
**#Bluebird Population in Dire Straits, Experts
     Predict**

Black Snake: When it wakes for the season, warmed in
       its over-
winter den, it will be very hungry.
Ears, barely seen by humans,
are tuned to the faintest sounds
as it makes its way through

weeds to the bird house,
it will appreciate a forthcoming meal.
The snake, the nestlings do not know
each other. Appreciation is not mutual.
Snakes when they coil,
do they work clockwise or
counter-clockwise.
**#Black Snakes Hunt Humanely, Recent Study
Shows**

People: We see harmless beings thrive in the sun and
we want to
save all the prey.
We are top predators
and like prey we appreciate
the sun; but among all three,
this appreciation is one-directional.
Take the election process,
for example: The candidates and
the rest of us appreciate the sun.
None is us knows
each other. We could get burned
easily enough. Sun wouldn't know
or care. Not unlike some top
predators who vie for the utmost spot,
thinking they have the best view.
**#Local Politicians Gather on Beach to Discuss
Climate Change**

Waste Land

Elizabeth Doyle Solomon

(Second place, *Skyline* Summer contest, 2016)

All week long log trucks have rumbled,
from those woods tall trees have tumbled—
hundred acres of limbs or more
have mourned in a dirge past my door.

Nests for our birds, shade for the deer,
two centuries' trees cut down clear—
cash for estate sold, taxes paid,
gashes in nature's beauty made.

Wife laid in her grave five years past,
a pall upon *his* grim face cast—
of their eight children just one near
Who knows why, but he watched trees cleared.

His siblings are spread, mostly far,
chose not to see their dad's falling star—
but see them return, bickering,
dividing silver, Judas-thing.

And so it goes, parents ignored,
until they're dead, life's trappings floored—
antiques, china, and children's toys
auctioned off amidst strangers' noise

Not many loved this sour man;
with pessimists, not many can—
did he deserve such apathy,
not one daughter, son's sympathy?

Cash from cutting all that timber
pays the costs while old man lingers—
bound by his bed-rails, soaking clothes,

hundreds like him, abandoned those.

In his dreams he'll hear the thrush
whistle from woods where winds once brushed—
his soul scarred like the land now bare,
his mind barren and unaware.

Lessons from Oenothera

Elizabeth Doyle Solomon

Bill brought me a full bouquet
of yellow oenothera blooms—
no one had ever told him that
they wilt when cut, each lov'ly plume.

Just minutes later in water
set before me in a green vase—
my husband's considerate gifts
all hung down, each sad drooping face.

Learn this then from oenothera:
some flowers are meant to admire
there in the garden where they grow.
Dare snip them and they expire.

The Oak Tree's Swing

Elizabeth Doyle Solomon

Both my grandchildren loved to sit
on the rope swing seat and be pushed
by Grandma. But that stout old branch
in the red oak tree was quite dead.

"Leave the swing but cut the dead branch,"
I suggested to Bill, who agreed.
With a muscular motion he sawed
back and forth with his dad's rope saw
flung high over the old dead branch—
Until it crashed down with a bang.
the rope swing stayed, and my heart sang!

Summer's First Firefly

Elizabeth Doyle Solomon

The first firefly appeared
on my window screen tonight—
he flickered for a moment
so that I might see his light.

He's like that first flashing spark
when God touched each spirit-soul—
that state of efflorescence
when our body flowered whole.

Little flying flicker-light,
you descended from the skies—
to touch my world a moment,
the way God does with His eyes.

Shenandoah Sunset

Elizabeth Doyle Solomon

Crimson streaks the sky
over Shenandoah's high—
stripes of mauve and peach
much farther than mountains reach.

Wind whips an old tree,
oak leaves over Bill and me—
and as we both looked,
lights twinkled in valley's nook.

Sunsets go so fast,
like lifetimes they do not last—
they sink into Time,
survive in just paint or rhyme.

July Gifts

Elizabeth Doyle Solomon

All in one day, gifts from my garden,
a profusion of colors and shapes!
Fourteen bright orange double-daylilies:
rising from green stalks, what fire each makes!

Proud pink phlox and white flowering spurge,
magenta bee balm, catnip's scalloped heads—
black-eyed Susans both sides of the gate,
and in its own pot, wild garlic's wine reds.

I need not walk farther than out the door,
for summer's beauties gazing at me—
all knowing their God-given duties,
each flower a jubilant joy to see!

Verses for Orlando

Phyllis A. Duncan

(Second place poetry, Blue Ridge Writers Chapter contest, VWC, 2016)

1. The Wife

I am your virgin here on earth, but I
told you in paradise there will be more.
One of them may do what I could not: Make
you a man. Instead of kisses, I hand
you some masculinity in a box.
Bullets for Allah, you will say, but I
simply wanted you to be a man. What
you wanted, we do not know beyond veiled
glimpses in social media or gay
dating sites; 911 calls for ISIS.
You wanted our son to grow up in a
safe country, as you had. How safe is he
now after you killed forty-nine people?
Not virgins, perhaps, but a sacrifice
on your father's dark altar of manhood.

2. The Gun Salesman

When I was a New York City cop I
saw what they did on 9/11. They
buried my brother officers in fire
for their pussy god. We made them pay with
Shock and Awe's vengeance. Make us great again
by banning rag heads from America.
Send them back to their camels and sand, but
if you still feel unsafe, perhaps my cold
inventory can help you. My store's a
Muslim-free zone for real Americans
to buy real guns. Didn't you see the sign
when you walked in? More than the sanctity

of the 2nd Amendment, money is
my god, worshipped on my dark altar of
manhood, my inalienable right.

3. The Alligator

If my brain were larger than three olives,
I might understand. Pleistocene instinct
is all that moves me. Offer me food, I
will strike, grasp, submerge. Stow tomorrow's meal
in mud and silt. Lurk in shadows, waiting
until my olive brain registers the
decomp. The tiny thing is no more than
an appetizer, but I mark it so
no rival A. Mississippiensis
steals my tender, sweet morsel. Food is food,
and didn't they realize the water's
edge is where I hunt? Five brothers and I
stalked, hunted, and captured. Sacrificed to
deflect responsibility, killed on
the dark altar of manhood's need to blame.

Untouchable Garden

Leonard Tuchyner

(Third place poetry, *Skyline* Summer contest, 2016)

To touch dark, moist, rich soil
nurtured to its loamy life
through decades of summer seasons,
with these toil hardened hands,
here in our land of the Piedmont
is to cherish and to be loved
by Mother Earth's soul and breast.

This year my body cannot bow
in this humble sacred communion,
to reach down from my bending knees,
and scoop sacred fragrant soil,
in expression of mutual love.
For my worn knees were stiff and sick.
Now changed from naked bone to plastic,
and the earth lies too far away.

My true strong friend has tilled it for me,
a gardener after my own heart,
though more chummy with machinery.
He does this as a gift of caring.
In return, I accept his selfless gift.
But to tell the truth, I suffer my loss
more, seeing him do what I so sorely miss,
watching someone else who is able,
doing that of which I am unable.
I respect and honor his need to give,
but it's painful for me to go too close.

So now my garden has two lovers,
as I give her to a man who can,
with a gracious show of gratitude,
hoping that next year in Virginia,
I will caress my waiting garden.

Grace Merritt

Joy Merritt Krystosek

(Third place poetry, Blue Ridge Writers Chapter contest, VWC, 2016)

I walked past the *Cinnabon* store at the mall
and for just a moment   thought I was
back in my great-grandmother's kitchen
the passage of time has had no effect
on my reminiscing of our favorite things

Days spent running in and out of their house
aromas from the kitchen driving us wild
anticipation of *cinnamon twister donuts*
still piping hot from the oil in the pan as she
          fished them out   rolled them in sugar
          lined them up on a rack to cool
as we waited eagerly to get a bite
couldn't steal them early
great-grandma was the *kitchen general*
we swore she had eyes in the back of her head

She wiped her hands on a freshly starched apron
worn over her faded cotton housecoat
ironed to perfection   hanging loosely
from her 100-pound frame

The heat from the kitchen didn't dampen her spirits
she hummed a tune from her favorite hymn
its melody mixing with the whir of the ceiling fan

She pushed back a single strand that slipped
from her braided and knotted bun where
sunlight hit to reflect the silver threads
woven by time throughout her hair

She puffed on her unfiltered *Camel* cigarette

as it hung from the right side of her mouth
its untapped ash grew longer as it bowed
perilously down towards the pastry sheet

Just as we thought it would drop onto
the batch of rolled dough
she would open her apron pocket with one
gnarled finger and flip the ash right in

We screamed in delight as we ran out the back door
she howled with laughter   swatted us with her
freshly ironed kitchen towel
and in her gravelly voice yelled
don't slam the screen door, dammit

She headed to her ironing board
to dampen the cotton sheets with a
water-filled Pepsi bottle topped with a sprinkler cork

She puffed on yet another unfiltered *Camel* cigarette
as it hung from the right side of her mouth
its untapped ash grew longer as it bowed
perilously down towards the perfectly ironed sheets

To Know the Heart

Stanley A. Galloway

(Second place, Elizabeth Neuwirth Memorial Contest, Poetry
Society of Virginia, 2016)

After Enrique Simonet y Lombardo's Anatomía del corazón, 1890

When I behold that heart I thought I knew
before, can I discern what words you held
unsaid? Anatomy can never hope
to track emotion's wisps unhoused today:
the light and dark foreshortening the facts,
the fancies, chiaroscuro of a heart
embarrassed to be glad except in hushed
and private moments, solitary tick
of joy for every hundred hours of
propriety. How many yeses beat
behind each no? This world of black and white
obscures the subtleties hearts harbor, mine
and yours, del Sarto to Lucrezia, dumb,
imagined whistles lancing syllables
from air before the ear can claim them. False
and true revolve like subject, object, and
subjunctive struggling for ascendancy.
No scalpel can reveal what motivates
this muscle of resistance, cleave its c's
and e's to truth, no sponge absorb its dew
of penetration—silent syntax. In
the sterile aftermath I hold your heart
as never in your life. Who better than
the one who vowed affection even as
you chose another—motioned me aside—
you cannot ask who is the savage, who
the noble, never knowing which stands by
you in the end. To know the heart is moot,
the spark and heft of romance starkly lost.

Canadian Prairie Gothic

Stanley A. Galloway

(Honorable mention, Ekphrastic Poetry Award, Poetry Society of Virginia, 2016)

After Grant Wood's American Gothic, *1930*
For Jenna Butler

> what is true about this land is not
> in mother-in-law's tongue or caladium
>
> cardboardy walls oiled against the wind
> home-shaped boards warping to old wood
>
> one ogival window pointing
> to sunbreak, windbreak
>
> carpenter-farmer who would have been a better dentist
> Sister Jones in cameo or gingham
>
> hayfork in one hand, calloused hopes in the other
> spreading straw and heritage on 640 acres
>
> forcing bloom, or green, from dust-soaked plots
> coaxing hard red wheat from dark soil
>
> one thin beaver pelt covering a cracked spindle
> weather whistling of Autumn chaff and winter ballast
>
> shadows grant peace
> faces long in the wind

Pond Dance

Stanley A. Galloway

(Honorable mention poetry, *Skyline* Summer contest, 2016)

where every moment is full // of the passion to keep moving
— "At the Lake" by Mary Oliver

Queen Anne's lace and dandelion
skirt the edge, shimmying
in sunlight, yellow and white
tight-legged and profligate.

Fat four-legged tadpoles
school green-brown against brown-green
learning that being oneself is
also becoming something else.

The water strider spread-eagles
where others flounder, sink
no more daring for doing
what no one told it it couldn't.

Wind rippling moment by eternal moment
(re)shaping, (re)heaping surface tension.

No name—like Walden or Golden—
just always slow-dancing
a rightness
its own raison d'etre.

I have my mother's lips, those she imparted upon her first of six

Lauvonda Lynn M. Young

(First place poetry, Appalachian Authors Guild, VWC, 2016)

*One of the greatest gifts you can get as a writer
is to be born into an unhappy family.*
— Pat Conroy

> I have my mother's lips,
> those she imparted upon her first of six.
>
> Mother's flawless lips, I could not love, since her viper
>   tongue lived inside. It
> was a tongue weighted by anger and depression, which,
>   fortunately, Mother
> failed to gift to me—although her acrid words did tell me I
>   was unloved.
>
> As I lurched into adolescence, my soul yearned for Dad to
>   stand by me, as an
> affirmation of love, but Father was a stone man, who
>   suffered abuses of his own,
> from the woman I called Mother—he called Wife. Perhaps
>   Dad thought me strong
> enough to fight my own battles, or maybe he could not
>   climb over his own. Many
> days after the sun wrapped itself in darkness, I wailed into
>   pillows, stopped
> dreaming about what could be, melted into books, slept
>   thereafter with reality.
>
> Time marched on—my parents aged. Disease struck:
>   Father bloated with a cancerous
> kidney, metastasized. Mother drowning in dementia and
>   strokes. They asked me to
> manage affairs, serve as caregiver. I became more mother

than daughter. We created a

new cadence. Love, under new management, befell all
    three. I realized affection and caring
arrive in diverse packages. My parents soon moved to
    eternal rest—I set about clearing their
lives from closets and scratched wooden drawers: family
    birth certificates; other documents
of value. There were stacks of tattered greeting cards, I
    mailed to Mother, over years. Many
bore imprints of her painted red lips. I chose to believe the
    kisses were a sign of aged love, so
I sealed my past in plastic tubs. Vowed to season with
    happiness, the future before me.

I have my mother's lips,
those she imparted upon her first of six.

I Remember

Lauvonda Lynn M. Young

Some memories are knitted to my soul—
    Often I am,
needled by images of the first time
    we made love,
in your decrepit Chevy, down at river's
    edge—Akin to adults,
I thought we were: me sixteen, you nineteen—
    There had been
ample talk of a future shared: so passion was
    unbridled—We sucked
words, from puffed lips, as trees, still robed in
    green, conversed with
stars—You became a wild stallion, me a
    flower, full-bloomed—
hunger sated: we dressed in silence, uneasy
    feelings already emergent—
For days your calls, were ignored, as I
    grappled with emotions:
cried for help, from Old Man Moon—
    When next we
met, you full of anger, spoke words,
    deplorable: The enormity
of my mistake, was exposed: the
    bestowing to you,
a gift I could bequeath once only.
              I remember

Petals in the Wind

Linda Levokove

In a forgotten long ago summer
just before the gilded twilight fell
we watched the sun pool red
til it succumbed to watery embrace . . .

after you gave me roses

Our fingertips tentatively touched
and we held our breath, made wishes
on that first falling star, although
I never told what I had wished for,
and now I can't recall.

I snip stems, carefully remove thorns
from this summer's bright blooms,
pondering how much is really true
in old memories and imagination,
or is it like the dead rose petals . . .

wafting in the wind

Fleeing as swiftly as a summer sunset
but still I wonder, if on some sultry night
do you ever look up at the star-filled sky,
close your eyes, and remember me?

Stealing Sweet Briar

Sigrid Mirabella

Prick my hand, Sweet Briar.
Sharp, your nettles pierce my heart.
Your breath so pink to bruise my soul. Rose,
you who plucks my air away with your small petals.
Pause me to moon for green rapture,
my breathless yesterdays.

Oh, dewy Mimosa, excite this night.
Fitful fragrance, lure me again
that I might dance dressed only in white honeysuckle,
my dappled braids swinging beneath starlight.
Here, have me hunt the shuttered day lilies
to touch their pure buds before day
coaxes from them their fleshy blooms.

Embrace me in my impatient hours, Mother Lilac,
your scent to still my eagerness. Restore
me to wonder the worth of ants and spider
          philosophies.
I beg your help to recall the stinging courtships
of woozy spring bees. Violets call out to them
with their spicy pollen, pray lust lasts forever.
Shall I weave a daisy crown for my head
and wait amid purple fields?

Prick my hands, sweet briar, that my bloody fingers
          carry you,
place you pink upon my wooden windowsill. Shame
me with your fading face that I dare to think
your wildness will live in glass and water.
Forgive my sin to steal you from thorns,
believe your pink can revive my own
while I watch your petals pale and wilt.
The scent lingers, nonetheless.

Let's Pretend

William E. Sypher

My mother died two years ago.
We buried her today,
an unspeakable delay.
She was still breathing
so we waited till she stopped.
Propped her up,
pretended we could talk.
It's the respectful thing to do,
is it not?

We just prolonged her death.
For whom, the bootless breath?
No hope of cure, or even slight reversal,
she just grew worse. This cursed
disease nibbled by degrees
but left her looking normal,
which put us at our ease.

Hospice staff with good intent,
smooth engines of disguising death,
hummed gracefully to the end,
but do the dying want such grace?
Do they like the game of "Let's pretend"?

We are what issues from our mind,
not from parts below it.
Heart to heart is little more
than lovely, mindless metaphor.
No gentler way to put it:
below the brain we do not jibe;
heart-lung machines do not describe
sensate conversations.

Having lost our word-forged links
in what sense do we live?

When our brains have gone so have we.
It's there for all to see, but we reject it
for a rising, falling chest, if we detect it.

Of the living we demand
a modest sensibility.
With the dying we conspire
to show it's not so burdensome
to talk for years with no reply that fits.
We prattle on in daily skits
loving, congenial lying.

PROSE NONFICTION

Fearless Flying

Susan M. Lanterman

"You can fly, you can fly, you can fly!" I howled at an excruciatingly high pitch as I flew circles around my parents' living room. It was a typical Saturday morning, and I was singing along to my favorite record, "Peter Pan." "Soon you'll zoom all around the room, all it takes is faith and trust . . . and a little bit of pixy dust!" I flew an endless loop, jumping from chair to ottoman to sofa, carefully not touching the floor, and thus falling from the sky to earth. It was the beginning of my fascination with flight.

Another weekend ritual involved rolling repeatedly down the hill of my minuscule front lawn. My friend, Johnny, and I then would lie on our backs at the bottom of the hill, prying our eyes open to look up to heaven—our heads still spinning. This rolling technique, coupled with the fast-moving clouds overhead, made us feel like we were levitating into the air. I remember wondering how many balloons tied at the waist it would take to float.

Eventually I convinced Johnny to try to launch me up into the air from a seesaw, with dismal results. I was undeterred. My goal as a six-year-old daredevil was to propel myself into the sky one way or another.

My most memorable flight plan involved my grandparents' old swing set. It was in the days when swing sets were never secured in cement. It was a personal challenge to make the legs pop in and out of the ground without toppling the whole thing over. During my weekend visits, I could monopolize the swing for hours. It was about my hundredth sway when I felt an uncontrollable urge. The air was swooshing at my back as I elevated myself dangerously high on the swing. My hind end was lifting off the seat and then slapping like a stone in a slingshot, ready to rocket out. The rusty legs were thumping excitedly in their holes, encouraging me upward . . . onward. And that's when I did it. I made the unreasonable decision to let go and "fly."

I didn't land on my feet like other kids did, hands raised in triumph. I let go the moment I had lifted slightly off the swing seat and could feel my weightlessness. What might happen next didn't even enter my mind. I propelled head first through the air and felt the momentary exhilaration. This thrill was quickly extinguished as I landed face first in the grass and dirt—dashing all hopes of a soft landing and a repeat flight.

"Whats'a matta for you?" I could hear my Sicilian grandmother bellow, as she scooped me up and carried me, crying, into the house. She couldn't help but grin as she picked the gravel from my hands and face.

My aviation experience was so abysmal I decided it was safer to just daydream that I was flying for a while. So, for many nights I would begin the process of falling asleep by imagining I was swinging on that creaky old swing set. After a few good pumps I was launched up and over the roofs of my nana's neighborhood, with that ticklish feeling in the pit of my stomach. I was able to look down at the rooftops from my swing, each time still holding on tightly to the ropes. I had, after all, learned one lesson in my quest for flight.

Having no fear of flying made me a willing victim to partake in the initiation ceremony of our neighborhood club. The final test of courage to enter the club was to scale a fence, climb on to our garage roof, and "jump" over a narrow alley to our neighbor's flat rooftop. The other potential victims were a few of the neighborhood kids who were younger than I was. Being the bravest and most foolish, I tied my jacket in a cape-like fashion around my neck and blazed a trail to attempt the impossible. I had climbed all the way to the top of the chain-link fence alongside the roof when I discovered I had hooked the back of my pants on the wire cross-pieces while trying to get my leg over the top. There was no going up and no coming down . . . with my pants on, that is. The humiliation of showing my Sunday best to an overly enthusiastic audience caused a delay in my flight plans. After tearing the pants off of the fence, I promptly took them to my mother and insisted that she sew them up so I could get on with the "'nitiation." Instead of an initiation, my flight was grounded for a week and never rescheduled.

It was Career Day in junior high when my future took wing. As unbelievable as it sounded, I found out I could become a stewardess and fly for free! At the time I was suffering from a bout of pimples, frizzy hair, and the lack of a major growth spurt. I wasn't exactly a prime candidate for what was considered a glamorous career. So I spent the next couple of years "getting experience" by taking advantage of the standby fares offered to anyone willing to sleep sitting up in a terminal while waiting for an empty seat on the next flight. I saved all my babysitting money and flew standby to visit anyone who put me up for a week. I was fearless and clueless.

As it turned out, I could never convince my parents that becoming a stewardess was more important than going to college. By the time I could earn my wings, the requirements to become a "flight attendant" had changed and my less-than-model looks would probably have passed. But I chose to explore other paths and I always flew to get there.

I was booked to fly to Europe on my honeymoon on September 23, 2001. Days before, I had watched the terrible scenes unfold on my computer at work and froze with fear. Images of a plane flying in the clear blue sky would normally be exhilarating, but now the sight was embedded in my mind with a new, frightening reality. Time stood still. We all stood still.

I didn't go on my honeymoon; in fact, I didn't go the year after either. We live in a different world now, I told myself, a world where low-flying planes give me pause and the thought of going on a business trip distressed me.

When I was a teenager I would travel with my friend, Tom. Tom's father would buy a life insurance policy for a couple of dollars at the airport each time his son traveled. We used to joke about it, but looking back it made me wonder why my parents didn't do it. Were they as confident as I was that flying was an adventure and not a risk? Would I now be grounded in fear of the unknown? Would I ever "believe" I could fly again?

The year I rebooked our flights to Paris and Rome, my husband and I finally drew up a will. Each time we took off and landed I closed my eyes and waited for that reassuring feeling . . . of my body rising slightly out of the seat and that weightless, ticklish sensation in the pit of my stomach. With each flight the anticipation of a new adventure swirled in my head. The tug of my seatbelt (holding me from lifting too far off of my seat) reminded me of the greater power that anchors us all in these uncertain times. Yes, that exhilarating feeling was still there and when I opened my eyes, I was still there. All it took was faith and trust. Save a little bit of pixy dust.

I can fly!

Trains, Planes, and Autobuses

Susan M. Lanterman

Americans are woefully resistant to public transportation. We are accustomed to being masters of our own destinations. So, when my husband and I began preparations to take various modes of transport across Italy, I experienced terror of the unknown.

I anxiously collected information about the locations of public transit, public parking, and, most important—public restrooms. Our dining room table was strewn with guidebooks, maps, and CDs as if we were about to launch a covert attack.

None of my planning revealed what I found on our bumpy road through Tuscany. Italy is a maze and you are the marble. So it's best to pick up your bags and roll with it. We survived our adventure—here's how we did it—no gelatos barred.

Upon disembarking at the airport in Rome, we were met by a pleasant-looking man inquiring politely if we could use an inexpensive transport. "*Naturalmente!*" we replied, missing the sign, "Do not accept rides in unofficial vehicles." We followed him to a shabby van. As the dented door slammed shut, I realized the road to Rome was probably paved with naïve tourists.

Groping for a nonexistent seatbelt, I clung to my hubby as we shot out on to the autostrade. Hell hath no fury like a driver in Rome. We came in for a landing in front of our hotel dazed and relieved. The cost of our ride was less than a cab ride, more than a train ticket, and the experience was—*priceless.*

We wisely chose a hotel near the center of the city. Although it was raining, my husband insisted that roaming by foot would give us the lay of the land. When you have to narrow your wardrobe to a glorified backpack on wheels, one should invest in sneakers and a waterproof poncho and say *arrivederci* to fashion.

We left all electronics home (for fear of being pillaged) and relied on old school maps. Circling concentrically, we hit

most of our targets, with the exception of the Pantheon—
Thomas Jefferson's inspiration for Monticello. Next we braved
the metro for a pilgrimage to the Vatican. As the door of the
metropolitana peeled open, it revealed travelers packed like
sardines. Claustrophobia be damned—we dove in.

Like Alice in Wonderland we were enticed with
choices: descend to the tombs, stroll the gardens or, my
husband's choice—climb to the top of the basilica. There was
an option to ride an elevator half way to the top of St. Peter's,
but he would not be enticed by convenience, so we climbed the
entire 550, or so, steps to the top. After conquering the
summit, we found the views were nothing short of *spettacolare*!

The next foray into public transportation was in a
tourist bus headed to Naples. As our bus winded its narrow
way up to the villainous Vesuvius, we chatted with the bus
driver and discovered it was his maiden voyage. Nearing the
top of the steaming precipice we were met by a line of buses
bearing down on us. Our driver's only choice was to back
down the rail-less mountainside. One slip and we too might be
buried in Herculaneum. At the base the passengers thundered,
"*Bravo*!!" as we checked that mode of transportation off our
list.

Our excursion to Florence would be by train. Finding
the right track to board seemed impossible. For this reason one
must have the phrase "Where is the train to Florence?" written
in Italian on the palm of your sweaty hand. Fortunately, the
information magically appeared just prior to the time we
needed to board.

Once in Florence we rented a car despite hearing
horror stories about wild Italian drivers. Having wheels allowed
us to speed like the plague throughout Tuscany and Umbria. At
week's end we had only one minor mishap. While a U.S. car
rental agency would have been picky, the Italian agency was
not—so when we returned the car a little *al denty*, it wasn't a
problem.

Before flying home from Rome, we took one last
sentimental ride around the city on the top of a double-decker bus
and from this vantage point we located the Pantheon. Be advised,
all roads and modes of transportation should lead you to Italy!

My Oklahoma Summer

Elizabeth Doyle Solomon

(First place nonfiction, *Skyline* Summer contest, 2016)

The summer before my sixteenth birthday, my father announced to us one morning at breakfast that we'd be taking a trip to Oklahoma. Muskogee born and bred on the wide prairie, where tumbleweeds and tornadoes swirled in summer and blizzards dumped snow in winter, my tall, tanned father had experienced it all.

"I want you kids to see the land where I grew up," Daddy explained. "You're city kids. It's all you've ever known."

Indeed, the four of us were New Orleans "crawdads," as comfortable in the black Delta mud and frequent rains as the crayfish for which Louisiana was so famous.

Our breakfast table exploded with questions. When would we leave? How long would we be gone? Who would care for Taffy dog and Susie cat?

Daddy laughed his deep bass laugh. "Whoa! Not all at once! Your mother and I are still working on the details. We have to make more calls to Uncle Jim in Tulsa and Uncle Bill in Oklahoma City. They're as excited as you are!"

We started to get up, each having a specific task in clearing breakfast. But Daddy stopped us—"What you *can* begin to do is to lay out two weeks of clothes. I'll get the suitcases from the attic today. Meanwhile, life goes on as usual: grass to cut, clothes to wash, and groceries to buy."

Three of us popped up like Jack-in-the-box, all except my baby brother, Farley, who was six months old and tied into his highchair. As the oldest, it was my job to tend to Farley. He babbled with his own incoherent excitement as I lifted his blond-haired, blue-eyed chubby self from the highchair.

"We're going to Oklahoma!" I told him as I wiped his face clean of baby food and changed his diaper. He smiled and cooed as if he really understood. I put Farley into his playpen and gave him some favorite soft toys.

My world was about to shift. I had to call my school friends and share the news. To say I was telephone-connected was an understatement. I pulled the black phone with the forty-foot-long cord into my bedroom and disappeared for an hour.

Daddy knocked on my door with his usual rat-a-tat knuckle message. I opened the door to find one huge suitcase, which my eight-year-old sister, Cindy, and I would share. Of course, I had to help her pack. My brother Paul, fourteen, could pick out his own clothes.

This was 1958, a time of considerable peace in our community. We never locked our suburban doors in Metairie, a quiet development along Lake Pontchartrain, where skunks and possums still visited and where hand-dug wells still supplied some homes with water. Sweet Mama had been dead for five years after fighting valiantly against cancer. Daddy always referred to our new stepmother as "your mother," even though we never felt comfortable calling her Mom. She was Nina to us and would be forever afterward.

Nina called me for another of my jobs on Saturday, hanging Farley's just-washed diapers on outside lines. During the week, Alice, our maid and housekeeper, did the cooking, cleaning, washing, ironing, and childcare. But on weekends, some of this fell to me. I lifted the heavy wicker basket and stepped outside, thick Bermuda grass cushioning my bare feet.

Six days later, on a typical hot and humid Friday in July, we were all ready to go—suitcases packed, Farley's six dozen diapers, rubber pants, a supply of canned formula and bottles with disposable plastic inserts, and baby food. I had spent two hours in our kitchen slicing ham down to the bone. I made a dozen ham and Swiss cheese sandwiches and a few extra PB&J ones for little sister Cindy. I filled a wicker hamper with paper plates, napkins, cups with our names printed with black marker, the sandwiches, cookies, and assorted fruit. I wrapped the big ham bone and froze it as a treat for Taffy when we returned. Neighbors would feed him and Susie cat while we were away.

We squeezed ourselves into the 1957 Chevrolet station wagon, Paul and Cindy bickering for a window seat. Jugs of juice and water filled the spaces beneath our feet, while suitcases were tied to the carrier on top.

Daddy handed me a small notebook. "Betty Ann," he said, "*you'll* be in charge of windows. Each of you will take turns. Your sister will write down the times, so there will be no arguing."

We were off with a last pitiful look from Taffy dog behind the gated fence, and Susie cat's demure pose from the front patio. Daddy took the newly completed I-10 Interstate west, over swamp lands, where herons and ibises stood statue-like, waiting to stab fish with their sharp beaks. Baby Farley slept a lot in his car crib. The whole family played our familiar games: "I spy something (name a color) . . . ," or "I packed my suitcase and put in . . ."—adding an object from each person, testing to see whose memories were best in remembering the most outlandish things, like a Volkswagen, clouds, a dinosaur, a ton of bricks.

My own favorite car-trip pastime was writing down license plates from passing cars to see how many states I could find. We stopped at noon for lunch at a well-shaded rest area with picnic tables in northern Louisiana. Spanish moss draped the trees, and Farley's baby-blue eyes reflected the summer sky.

At the state border, we stayed in a town with the names of three states, Texarkana, for Texas, Arkansas, and Louisiana. I could stand in the middle of that town and walk a few steps in any of three directions to be in each of these three states!

When we crossed the Arkansas River the next morning after breakfast, Daddy stopped to take pictures. "This river separates Arkansas from Oklahoma," he pointed out. "But look at the difference between *this* river and our mighty Mississippi." There was barely a trickle in its sandy bottom. We might have easily walked across.

"Pioneers like your grandma and grandpa who settled the West wanted several things: access to water, fertile soil, and neighbors at least three miles away. Your grandparents raised me and ten other siblings on a small piece of Oklahoma prairie, came west in a covered wagon from Kentucky. This territory didn't become a state until 1907. Your Uncle Haskell is named for the first governor of Oklahoma. Grandma buried two of us, or else you might have had more cousins than you do."

The land got dryer, hotter, and more barren as we sped through Oklahoma. We were used to the lush green trees and grasses of the Louisiana delta, but here the only color was along stream and riverbanks.

I was the first one to see an oil well, its big mouth pumping, pumping, up and down. Then there were so many that I lost count. "Black gold," Daddy explained. "It's what has made a lot of Oklahoma landowners rich. Oilmen come in and offer a farmer pretty big bucks for the rights to drill."

We crossed the Red River, this time not a trickle, but a swollen torrent, the waters red from the state's red clay. We sang all the songs from the musical *Oklahoma!* in which I'd had a part, singing in the chorus. I had played the LP record so many times that the family knew most of it. I especially liked the lead piece:

"We know we belong to the land
And the land we belong to is grand!"

Where there weren't oil wells, there were miles of cornfields and sunflowers, with a windmill at every farmhouse. I could not write fast enough about what I saw. These notes would turn into articles for my school paper, where I was features editor, or into poems of what would become thousands over the years.

We stopped at fast-food restaurants along the way, but we always chose shady spots for picnics, usually beneath the numerous cottonwood trees along stream sides. Their beautiful leaves, whispering in the ever-present prairie winds, have a magic for me until this day.

As we neared the big population centers of Tulsa and Oklahoma City, Daddy stopped to find a pay phone to call Uncles Jim and Bill. These were pre-cell phone days. We couldn't imagine what a revolution they would create in thirty years as we brought up our own children. I forgot the name of that town—just a blink and it's gone—but what I'll always remember was a cowboy on his horse who cantered up to a drive-in liquor store. He bought a quart of whiskey, stowed it in his saddlebag, and was about to gallop away when he saw me with my camera. He waved his big gallon hat and smiled at me!

We drove first to Tulsa, where Uncle Jim and Aunt Merle lived. They had no children, but they had made a child of their ancient black cat. Old Black Joe (after the Stephen Foster song) was toothless, deaf, nearly blind, and twenty-two years old. He slept most of the time, but his nose was still working fine, even asleep.

We six travelers gathered on an open-air patio with Daddy's oldest brother, his wife, and Old Black Joe. Uncle Jim had inherited my grandpa's building and stonemason skills. He had poured the cement floor himself and had bricked-in a barbeque pit. Born in 1898, Uncle Jim's eyes at sixty were as good as mine. He wore no glasses and pointed out various stars and constellations in the clear Oklahoma night sky. Hot dogs and chicken slow-cooked on the pit's grill, and Black Joe's nose started wiggling.

Aunt Merle saw me petting her old cat, and said, "Follow me, Betty Ann." We went into their low-slung home, with its Spanish-style roof and doors. It was surprisingly cool, with Indian blanket drapes on the windows and rattan mats on the ceramic floor. Aunt Merle took a can of cat food from the pantry and opened it. "Just put this under Black Joe's nose and see what happens."

When I set the opened can of cat food next to Black Joe's head as he lay stretched on the cool concrete, his nose woke up first, twitching and wiggling. With a loud purring-meow from his worn-out vocal chords, his pink tongue started lapping soft food.

We stayed that first night in Uncle Jim and Aunt Merle's cool home. At breakfast, Daddy and Uncle Jim were already making plans for the drive to Muskogee, about thirty miles to the south past small towns whose names captured my vivid imagination as they rolled off Uncle Jim's tongue. Paul and I rode with my uncle and aunt through Broken Arrow, Wagoner, and Tullahassee.

Muskogee had grown from a pioneer town in the early 1900s to a good-sized city in sixty years. It was about 40,000 people. Grandma and Grandpa's farm was south of Muskogee, near where the present-day Sequoyah River graces the state park of the same name. The little house that my grandpa's hands had built was still standing, with a lean-to for firewood and an old well with a hand-turned pulley for the bucket. Grandpa's barn and chicken coop still stood too, with tumbleweeds blown against the barnyard fence.

"Remember that Holstein cow we took turns milking?" Uncle Jim asked my father. "I was the oldest, and I taught you how to milk, Paul." Daddy scratched his head, recalling those years. "Yeah, Bossy decided I wasn't doing it right, and she kicked over the bucket."

Uncle Jim led us away from the house to a lone cottonwood tree. Beneath its branches were two markers set into the prairie soil. One was inscribed "Celia Mae Doyle, 1905," and the other simply said, "Baby Doyle, 1905." I knelt down near the stones, touching them as if to fathom how my grandma had handled so much tragedy and sorrow in such a short time. Although I was there nearly sixty years ago, the names are etched into my memory.

"Celia died of diphtheria during the blizzard of January, 1905," Uncle Jim remembered. "She was just five years old and there was no vaccine for it then like there is today. We kids watched from the loft as Mom laid snow-cloths on Celia's forehead, which was burning with fever. Mom had tried all of her home remedies from plants we helped her to pick in the summer months. Dad saddled one of the wagon mares and rode to Tulsa in that raging snowstorm. What would normally have taken sixty minutes on a fast horse, took him over two hours. When the doctor came back with him, he told my mom that there was nothing in his black bag that would cure diphtheria. Mom gave him a warm bowl of vegetable soup and wrapped a loaf of her fresh-made bread in oil cloth to put in his saddle bag. In those days, you gave *what* you could and paid *when* you could."

"What about the stone that just says 'Baby Doyle'?" I asked Uncle Jim. Daddy spoke up as if all of it were suddenly coming back to him. "I'll never forget the night Celia Mae died. A bright light beamed into the house where no oil lanterns were lit. It moved around the room three times and then stopped at Celia Mae's bed. A voice came out of that light, but none of us were afraid. It was strangely calming."

Uncle Jim continued when Daddy's words seemed to choke in his throat. "The voice said, 'I'm taking Celia Mae to a far better place tonight, where she will never know pain again. And in two weeks, Flossie, I'm taking your unborn baby. But you will have many more children, and dozens of grandchildren.'"

It was Uncle Jim's voice that seemed to crack now. My father continued. "Celia Mae died several hours later, and in two weeks, Mom delivered a stillborn baby with the help of an Indian midwife who had aided many pioneer women in the area. The ground didn't thaw until April, so we boys and Dad had time to make two small coffins from an old dead cottonwood that we helped Dad cut the summer before."

Although we did spend time in Oklahoma City with my Uncle Bill and Aunt Sue and their two boys, it was the time in Tulsa and Muskogee that impressed me the most. After we returned to New Orleans, I asked my grandma why she had never spoken about those hard times of 1905. She gave me a wise answer.

Then in her eighties, she explained, "Don't cry over the past. Those tears are dried and gone. Always look to the future, Betty Ann. Keep your faith, and it will make you strong for whatever happens."

Indeed, that Oklahoma summer, the Muskogee tombstones, and my grandma's words, have become the bricks of my strength. I wanted ten children like Grandma, but lost two, one stillborn like hers. Grandma died in her sleep at the ripe old age of ninety-three, but she lived to see my two adopted babies, one who I named Florence for her. And far away, the prairie dust and tumbleweeds of Oklahoma still call to me.

The Execution, Riyadh, Saudi Arabia

William E. Sypher

(First place nonfiction, Blue Ridge Writers Chapter contest, VWC, 2016)

Unlike magnetic city squares in other world capitals, Dirah Square in Riyadh attracts no painters or poets. It is simply a sprawling ten-acre parking lot whose only notable features are a large mosque on its western edge and a twenty-five-foot-high clock tower on its eastern side. This calm sea of gray, oil-splattered asphalt belies its purpose. At the base of the clock tower, executions are carried out on Fridays, shortly after noon prayers. Executions are punctual, probably the only event in the culture that is, in the view of expatriates who joke about such things. Expats laughingly refer to the site as Chop Chop Square, distancing themselves from the awful finality of what occurs there.

Within a month of my arrival in Saudi Arabia, word trickled out—the usual way of news in a country with a tightly controlled press—that on the coming Friday, two Saudi football players on the national team were to be beheaded for raping a Saudi woman. They had gotten drunk, so the story went, which, in this teetotaling state, added a dash of explanation for such a rare and unspeakable act. Drunkenness is intolerable and virginity for unmarried women is required, so two virtues had been trampled simultaneously. The spectacle of a double execution was sure to draw a massive, noisy crowd.

I decided to witness the execution, not out of any morbid fascination for seeing someone die, nor out of any need to stiffen my resolve to obey the law and avoid this horrific end, but rather to evidence and confirm my opposition and revulsion at cold-blooded state killing. Still, I felt guilty at the thought of going there as I headed down narrow Suaylum Street two blocks to the square.

Two weeks earlier, a Palestinian friend, Noor, had driven me to the precise site of an execution in the square, a few hours after the fact. Cars had pulled back in, filling up the parking lot. Between two cars a few feet from the base of the clock tower was a small pool of dark red blood not yet dried and a white, round lace cap, the *taqiya*, which Muslim men wear under their cloth headpieces, *ghutras*. Once dried, the blood would be just another spot among many oil and grease spots on the asphalt. The site of the execution had no more significance than any spot on any stretch of asphalt anywhere in the universe. Something elemental and irreversible had happened there a few hours earlier, something designed to induce fear into the spectators, to deter them from criminal acts that would cause them to lose their heads. One would have thought the spot would have been marked in some way, roped off, even temporarily, to serve as a reminder of the power of the State, but it was not and never would be. The audience had gone home. The theater was dark. It was an event at once cosmic for the victim and inconsequential for history.

Sayeed al-Saif has served as the official Saudi executioner for over forty years, cutting off his first head when he was twenty-three, for which he earned $133. Six hundred more heads fell under his razor-sharp sword over the years. He is utterly unemotional about his job, seeing it simply as a way of making a living and of defending God's Law. Asked by a Jeddah journalist if all the victims die immediately, he replied, "Most of them. Very few need another hit, and rarely is a third necessary." Sayeed has groomed his son, Mohammed, to take over for him.

Around 10:00, two hours before the execution, and still uneasy about going, I strolled leisurely down the street to the square, pausing to look in shop windows, wanting to appear as if I had just come upon the scene by accident. It was a pointless ruse. Who would notice or care? I could hear the hum of a large crowd as I approached. Ringing the square were cars and trucks crammed with spectators. Some had climbed out onto the roofs of the vehicles for a better view, denting them. Whose cars? No matter. Others had even crawled onto the canvas-canopied roofs of pickup trucks that haul workers; their weight had caused the canvas to sag and then rip. Did the truck owners care or were they too fixated on the coming spectacle to notice? No matter, today was an execution;

spectacular death was in the offing. Normal sensibilities could be put on hold for a while. The balconies of multistory buildings on two sides of the square were jammed with onlookers, some sitting precariously on the railings. Others, not well-enough connected to gain a balcony perch, had shinnied up lampposts and climbed up the sides of the clock tower itself, where they looked tenuously stuck on like postage stamps. One might have expected a somber crowd, grimly anticipating that justice would be served for the unspeakable crime. Instead, the mood was festive. Had anyone come by selling balloons or popcorn or splashy color programs, no one would have thought it amiss. The assembled had come for theater, a morality play; they were hardly obliged to adopt grim faces when entertainment was on tap.

In the midst of the great swarm of five thousand men, a cube-shaped black van emerged from a side street and pushed slowly through the crowd. Led by a dozen policemen with rubber truncheons who frantically struck the legs of the curious swarm, the van inched through the sea of spectators, spreading them at an acute angle like water parted by the bow of a boat, and like water, the crowd immediately filled in behind the van. Finally the van made it to within thirty feet of the clock tower and stopped. Two burly policemen got out and went around to the back, presumably to unlock the doors. The mob pressed in, feverish to get a close-up view of the doomed monsters. Would this crowd, ravenous for justice, try to administer its own punishment and brutally separate limbs from the condemned men's bodies before the executioner would coolly and clinically separate their heads?

A larger group of policemen circled the van and began to thrash the mob even more vigorously, causing them to turn and run wildly. From my vantage point, maybe fifty feet from the clock tower, it was as if a great hole had opened up in the center of the plaza, where the van now stood alone, a kind of squat, black monument in a giant circle approximately two hundred feet in diameter, where hundreds of rubber and leather sandals and red and white checked headscarves were scattered about, left by the madding throng as it fled to escape the beatings.

After some time, the crowd grew impatient and began slowly, almost imperceptibly, to close in on the van. The police took little notice; they seemed relaxed and confident they had the throng under control. The execution could proceed as scheduled. But this one was not on schedule. Perhaps some last-minute legal maneuvering was holding up the show, but in Saudi Arabia that seemed unlikely. Death sentences are approved by a succession of courts up to the Supreme Court of Cassation; the possibility of legal maneuvers at this stage seemed remote indeed. Whatever doubts any judge harbored about guilt or degree of guilt would have been dealt with long ago. The explanation must be elsewhere and perhaps mundane. Could the executioner have been caught in traffic? Were certain officials of the police or a mosque required as witnesses detained by other business?

The horde pressed ever closer like a sea ready to swallow a helpless, wallowing boat. At some point the invisible circle around the van, which the police were prepared to defend, must have been breached and the police stormed into the crowd, which fled as before, leaving in its wake more sandals and *ghutras*. The empty circle was now back at a manageable two hundred feet in diameter, and the crowd stared at the van and at the police. Now one hour past the scheduled execution time, the assembled grew restless for action and began again to shrink the diameter of the protective circle. A few shouts from the policemen deterred them momentarily but the momentum was too great and, as with most mobs, the push comes from the emboldened ones safely shielded from the police truncheons by those on the front line, who turned around angrily and shouted at the throng that was pushing them. Once again the safety circle had shrunk to the danger point and the police attacked, this time with greater fury, with truncheons flying indiscriminately and the mob receding.

Over the next hour this scene was repeated three more times until murmuring among the crowd grew louder and louder and with shaking heads, they started to disperse, filling the side streets around the square. What caused them to leave was a rumor that a prince had intervened at the last moment and had commuted the rapists' sentences to life. They were renowned football players after all, and the Saudi national team had been inching toward world recognition. The national image could not be tarnished by the news that two of its stellar athletes had been executed.

If such theater as was performed that day could be reported freely in the entertainment pages of the local newspapers, the stories might begin with something like: "The ritual of public execution falls far short as a morality play." Critics would pan it as too melodramatic, too self-righteous, too predictable. But what happened there on that day departed from the script, infusing it with uncharacteristic drama.

From the Saudi perspective, public executions lead to safer streets, especially for women, and an ultralow murder rate. The connection between crime and punishment is clear to them and justified by the Quran. That their low crime rate might just as well result from having a largely homogeneous population with strong clan and family links and fervent religious principles does not seem persuasive to them. They are unwilling to test this proposition by granting a moratorium on execution.

Unlike the disappointed throng, I did not walk away from Dirah Square unfulfilled. I was glad not to have witnessed society's bloody reprisal. I cannot countenance the icy, deliberate taking of a life by the State. It serves no purpose other than revenge, one of humankind's most primitive emotions. If it could deter the bestiality now so prevalent in modern societies, that would argue in its favor, and I would have to reconsider my position. But evidence for deterrence does not exist. When Charles Dickens went up to Tower Hill where a pickpocket was about to be hanged, he noted, to his horror, that pickpockets were busy fleecing the spectators. States in the United States that have introduced capital punishment have not experienced a decrease in murder; states that abandoned it have not witnessed an increase. In short, there is no relation between capital punishment and the incidence of capital crime and the reason is obvious: the overwhelming majority of those who murder do so impulsively with no forethought about punishment.

One could even argue, like Norman Mailer, who interviewed several hundred inmates on Death Row, that such a violent, spectacular punishment can even be seductive to those who have lived their lives in a spirit of violent retribution and who are excited by the thought of such an end, as opposed to dying quietly and unheeded in a gutter somewhere. Gary Gilmore, whose life Mailer chronicled in *The Executioner's Song*, was just such a man. His last words to the Utah firing squad: "Do it!"

For lesser crimes in Saudi Arabia, like repeated theft, amputation of a hand is carried out, but this is not done theatrically at Dirah Square, but in hospitals, where doctors must choke on the part of the Hippocratic Oath that binds them to do no harm, as they saw off a perfectly good hand.

Still a Mountain to Go

Leonard Tuchyner

(Second place nonfiction, *Skyline* Summer contest, 2016

Sweat is running down my face in a torrid downpour, as I make my weekly bicycle jaunt from Harrisonburg to Greene County. I've covered fifteen miles of the forty-mile distance, and the midsummer sun still has three hours before it hits its zenith in Virginia's Shenandoah Valley. "This is crazy," I tell myself. I've been doing this trip for over three years on Rt. 33, through every imaginable and unimaginable weather, from blizzard to pavement-melting hellish heat, like today. There's got to be a better way from here to there. Well if there is, I haven't found it. They won't give me a driver's license because I'm legally blind, and I don't want one. I'd rather face a rampaging black bear than someone like me behind the wheel of a car. Part of my psychotherapy practice is in Harrisonburg, on the west side of the Blue Ridge Mountains, and the other part is in Ruckersville, on the east side.

At the moment, the thought of pedaling up that mountain in this heat is not comforting me. I take another pull on my water bottle, realizing that water is pouring out of me faster than I'm putting it in. Why, oh why, did I forget to fill the second bottle?

Sounds of a farm tractor punctuate this torrid summer morning. I glance to my left, across the highway, and spot it chugging away in a grazing field that is still shadowed by Massanutten Mountain. "Smart farmer," I think. In another three hours, that field is not any place a sane person would want to be running a midsized tractor. Or, for that matter, pedaling a mountain bike on a heat-trapping blacktop highway. So he must be sane, and I must be out of my mind. I have the credentials to back up my diagnoses.

Automatically, I stay to my right, as my right becomes a turn lane. It's not that I want to turn into the small industrial park where it leads. It's just that more than once, a car or truck has passed me on the right in such a lane, thus stranding me between two streams of deadly traffic. However, my tactics didn't work two weeks ago.

Despite the fact that I was occupying this small stretch of lane, a car veered into that road, ignoring the rule that two objects cannot occupy the same space at the same time. Since the vehicle outweighed me by a couple of tons, I found myself heading horizontally into the tarmac. On my way to that dark destination, I screamed to get the driver's attention. When she finally realized she had just run into a strange fellow on two wheels, she stopped, satisfyingly alarmed at her questionable driving skills. She was shook up and blitheringly apologetic. I was pissed off, but basically unscathed.

"I'm sorry. I'm oh, so sorry. Are you okay?"

"I'll live. How the hell did you not see me? I'm flying a danger flag, wearing a bicycle orange vest, and I have florescent stripes on my helmet."

"Oh, I'm so ashamed. I was distracted by my children in the backseat and wasn't watching the road. Can I take you to a hospital?"

"NO ma'am. Not today. Thankfully, I'm fine, but my bike's wheel seems a little bent."

"Can I at least drive you somewhere?"

"Not unless you have a bicycle carrier."

"We could put it in the trunk," she persisted.

"No we couldn't. It won't fit. I have a friend I can call who has a carrier. But you can pay me for damages to my bike. Give me a few minutes and let me check it out."

"I'm so sorry."

I rolled my eyes and ignored her, as I set my steed on its back and tested the front wheel. "Yeah, it will need a new wheel and truing. Thirty bucks ought to cover it."

"Are you sure that's all. Are you okay?"

"I'll be fine." Most of my mood had lightened, but she was driving me to severe annoyance at her oversolicitousness. I was beginning to feel twice the victim. She was trying to absolve herself of guilt at my expense. It had occurred to me that I could oblige her by insisting that we wait for the police to come. She'd get a ticket for reckless driving and feel completely absolved of her guilt, having paid for her sins. But that was only my sarcasm thinking. Besides, I'd have to go to court as a witness. I had better things to do.

Well, that was two weeks ago, so why am I perseverating about it now? Another five miles and I'll be at the foot of the Blue Ridge. Every time I pedal up those switchback slopes, I gear up too high. Today will be different. I'll get as much mechanical advantage as I can and spin my cranks without effort. Right now, I have to concentrate on my rhythm for the flatlands. The only breeze around is the one I'm making by cutting through the hot, still, stagnant air. Time to stand up in the stirrups and take the pressure off my crotch, change my handholds, and get low over the elbow rests. "Pace yourself, pace yourself."

I'm getting light-headed. Don't remember feeling that way before. I must be dehydrating, but there's no more water. It's only two miles to a convenience store at the mountain's base. I'll buy three bottles of Gatorade and soak my system. It'll be all right.

Finally! I've made it. I hitch up my bike and enter the convenience store, feeling faint and sick to my stomach. "What's wrong with me? I can hardly stand up. I've never felt so close to fainting in my life. Ah, at least the store is air conditioned." It revives me a little. I make my purchase and can't wait to slurp down a bottle. I go back outside into the heat and find a place to sit down and guzzle. I finish off the first Gatorade almost without swallowing. Slowly, the dizziness lightens. I was afraid I was having a heart attack, but I'm on my way back. Not a heart attack, just dehydration. So this is what sunstroke is all about. Miraculously, within twenty minutes, I feel normal and ready to climb to the top. But first I go back into the convenience store and stock up with two more bottles of Gatorade and pour the contents into my sports bottles. Then I place them in their mounted holders. After all, I still have twenty miles to go.

"Smarter, easier, no hurry" is my new motto. Only it doesn't turn out that way. This new motto is actually my old motto that is resurrected every time I make this trip. I've got to go five miles to the top, and within half a mile it's the same familiar, muscle-straining grind. But this verdant mountain shades most of the road as it twists in its elongated Ss.

The sheer rock and open drop-offs are spectacular. In some places, bare granite parapets are close enough to the road that I can almost touch them from my bike. The overlooks aren't simply majestic naked rock. Verdant tapestries of vegetation cascade down them in the form of thick forests. This is an ancient, ancient worn mountain that never rises completely above the tree line.

After three miles I stop to rest at my usual place. I gaze down into the Shenandoah Valley. The view is restorative and helps me to understand why I continue to make this ride week after week.

The last two miles are the steepest and rockiest. I stand in the stirrups to bull my way up the cruel grade. Finally, I'm on the final straight runway to the crest, wherein lies an entrance to the Blue Ridge Parkway that runs all the way to Tennessee and the Smoky Mountains. I will rest at the summit and lean my bike against one of the great stone monuments that grace the summit. My spirits are buoyed up, knowing that it is almost all downhill from there.

As I approach the peak, a delightful surprise awaits me. Three mule deer stand placidly along the side of the road. They don't move away as I pass slowly by them. I know that deer here are protected by a no-hunting zone and are not afraid of people. Of course, bucks are timid, no matter what, and I'm not surprised that one is not seen with this small group. I wonder if a buck is hiding in the shadows of a nearby stand of trees and bush. What a privilege to experience the trust of the three does concerning my close presence.

I stop by one of the monument boulders to get off my bike and rest. A few deep gulps of still-cool liquid feel wonderful. I am slowly drawing closer to them, but I don't approach closer than ten yards. A human on foot is a lot different than one on a bicycle. Although, they don't move away, they are watching me alertly with their big brown eyes. They are facing the road, so only one eye for each is trained on me. Time passes quickly.

Eventually, it is I who must move on. Home is twenty miles away.

When I first started to make this trek three years ago, I looked forward to enjoying the free energy and speed that gravity would grant in the downhill plunge to the eastern mountain base. There would be nothing for me to do but steer. But I soon learned that this attitude was the voice of inexperience. A visually challenged rider can't safely go at breakneck speeds under any conditions. Nevertheless, I put knowledge and wisdom aside and welcome the deceptive grace of gravity. I can never resist a free ride, from sailboating to hitchhiking.

The euphoria hasn't lasted long. As the slope steepens and I face my first hairpin curve, I apply my hand breaks to keep my speed manageable. Any stone or stick in the road could mean doom, as I have oft discovered. I have no desire to run into a mountain cliff, or off one, for that matter. No shortcuts for me, thank you.

Only about two minutes have passed, and gravity has become a wild beast. My life depends upon keeping it from having its way. Already the constant pressure on my palms is making them ache. My fingers, which are maintaining obligatory pressure on the hand brakes, are tired. I must maintain a constant vigil on any visual inputs I can perceive. Speed is a dangerous temptress that could change my life or end it.

Finally, I reach the three-quarters mark, where the mountain takes a breather and flattens out. Dogpatch-style mountain dwellings look down upon me from their precarious perches. A quarter-mile stretch of small businesses runs along this straight, brief portion on the east side of the Blue Ridge. Then it ends.

I'm back wrestling with switchbacks and threatening descents. But this is the final plunge. Modest mountain dwellings are more plentiful. Gone are impressive cliffs and rock walls waiting to ensnare or dash me. My forearms, shoulders, and hands ache from constant pressure and fatigue.

I'm on the straightaway, which takes me into a relatively gently hilled area of Central Virginia. The sky is opened to me as all mountain shade is withdrawn like colossal window shades. The narrow, double-lane roadway opens up to a four-lane highway that bypasses Stanardsville, Greene County's county seat.

My cramped hands loosen their death grip on the brakes. My forearms relax into the handlebar extensions, and my shoulders slacken. My saddle angle is drastically changed as I slump into a low, streamline contour. I thrill to the speed, as I let go and let gravity have its way. Road debris is unlikely on this part of Rt. 33, so I trust in good fortune.

My bike coasts for several miles until it comes to a gentle stop. I dismount and leisurely enjoy a bottle of Gatorade. Home lies ten miles away. Without mountain altitude and shade, the day is hotter than it was on the western side of the Blue Ridge. The sun is almost at its zenith. But I feel refreshed and eager to complete this day's journey. There will be clients to be seen in my home office.

Just the same, I think back to a glorious late spring thunderstorm I pedaled through on this same route. It was frightening at the time, and I needed to get off the road. But today, with its swelter, it seems like a pleasant dream.

I remount, settling my abused crotch into the saddle, and head for home.

My Body as Evidence

Roger Tolle

(Second place nonfiction, Blue Ridge Writers Chapter contest, VWC, 2016)

For thirteen years, Michael and I had been more merged than most straight married couples I knew. We had one house, one car, one bank account, one set of friends. Our bedroom had one closet, with one set of clothes. We even shared just one drawer for underwear and socks. Separating now, with friendly finality, offered each of us a huge and welcome freedom to rediscover ourselves.

For me, pulling out the attachments to him and to his mundane dreams of two old men rocking peacefully on a porch, dreams that had taken root in my body as well as my mind, seemed both overwhelming and exciting. In two weeks new owners were to move into the house we had just cleaned out for them, and I had no clear vision of where I would go or what my life from then on would be about. I knew only that I would need to go inward for a while.

I needed to dive in and listen deeply. I needed to reconnect to what my Quaker heritage referred to "the still small voice within." This had always been a trusted and reliable guide for me, but in the bustle of domestic life, and especially in the intensity of the unsuccessful struggle to stay together with Michael, I could no longer hear it. Reclaiming my inner wisdom needed time. I knew that much. But how much time, and where I should be living during that time was not clear to me.

Where should I set up house to rethink my life, my path, my purpose? Where should I put myself in this world to do the work of demolishing the parts of my structure, the mental constructs that I no longer wanted holding me in place? Where should I sleep while dreaming up my next life story? Where should I stand while rebuilding the foundations of my life? Wherever I chose, I wanted to build it out of my own lived experience, my own body of evidence.

To figure all that out, I booked a week in a little summer cottage on the Outer Banks. Only $400, and right on the beach. The summer hordes were gone, and the storms of icy rain expected soon. Without insulation, the cottage was not an appealing shelter for any of the other usual beach goers, even those who like to roam the empty stretches of sand off-season. But for me, it was the perfect place to contemplate where I would rebuild my life.

* * * *

I listened to the wet sea air whistling through the cracks around the door with my feet propped up on the edge of the stove, the only heat source in the cottage. I was counting on the wind to blow through my mind, as well as through the cracks in the siding.

Listening to the insistent pulsation of the sea was exactly what I needed in order to drown out the echoes of my discontented dickering with Michael and his angry, driven efforts to right the wrongs of our physical environment. His voice was still woven into my mind. I needed the wintry blast to disentangle the warp of his dissatisfactions from the delicious weave of my sensory and emotional truths.

I needed wild and wind and waves and weather to erode the landscape of my thinking, thinking that I knew had been partially shaped in my flattened response to Michael's frustratingly depressed mood. So I bundled up for long tearful walks on the beach, facing directly into the gale with one mittened hand shielding my cheek from the slap of frozen spray.

I spent hours on those wide expanses of almost horizontal overlapping layers of sea, foam, sand, clouds, and color. This was not the stationary flatness of the Midwest where I grew up, but constantly shifting and flowing vectors of no more than 2 degrees slicing my sightline. This was thrilling and inspiring spaciousness.

I found myself thinking and feeling freely back and forth across the veil between inner sensory experience and the simple activities of each day. I played between outer activity and inner life like a child plays in the water and in the sand simultaneously. Just as I strode freely out to greet the rush of the surf as it carved new patterns into the shore, I greeted the rush of thoughts and sensations that were constantly changing the shape and texture of my emotional landscape.

I let the clean cold cut through me. Then, to keep warm, I savored hours under layers of covers in the high double bed with the ocean view. If a receding wave left a glassy surface on the smooth sand that reflected lavender and turquoise and mauve and silver from the sky, I painted sheets of sensory color onto my skin. I scanned my body for the texture and location of sensations and watched cautiously, but without holding on, as I made myself available for whatever was moving, whatever was wanting to let go, whatever was wanting to be rebuilt. Huddled inside heavy layers of clothes, I explored the random and patternless ebb and flow of micro-movements. I inhibited patterns of emotional habit, and rested my mind from the repetitive rethinking of the recently ended relationship. I untangled the overgrowth muddling my mind and ripped free the tendrils of gnarly restriction in my inner movement—restriction that was making my thinking rigid.

Here in this sound-washed cottage, I silently enjoyed each moment, sensation after sensation. I awakened oceans of tactile and kinetic treats. I told myself that this reemerging access to inner movement was exactly what I wanted to use to model my new life.

This new space in my mind felt inspiring—and hopeful too. But I needed much more time for this process of unwinding, and the rebuilding that would have to follow. I needed months, not days. And it became apparent there really wasn't a better place than back in Charlottesville, with its welcoming communities of artists and seekers, to do all the letting go and reinventing. So I headed back there to find myself an inexpensive, but sensually supportive, place to live.

* * * *

After looking at a few places in town, I settled, with the excitement of a four-year-old arriving at a new playground, on a sweet little cabin on the edge of an extensive rolling wooded acreage that was part of a sheep farm just fifteen minutes from town. I had budgeted enough of the money Michael and I had made on the sale of our house to carry me through six months of this place without needing to work in the world.

I still harbored an old fantasy that I would find peace inside if I could get to a place far enough away from human interruption, a place where aloneness was more powerful than loneliness. This cabin in the woods would not only be a sanctuary for the investigation of the experience of aloneness. It would be my experiment in being a hermit—not at the isolated edge of anything, but in the middle of Virginia, in the middle of a farm; and, I noted, exactly in the middle of my life.

The two-level cabin was set on a hillside, with the entrance on the upper level. Only two rooms fit on that level . . . a wood-paneled, sun-soaked living room with hardwood floors and windows on three sides, and a small but efficient kitchen. In between, the stairs down led to the wood stove that heated the place, and to two small rooms, one on either side. The smallest would just barely handle my full-sized mattress on the floor—no bed yet, as I wasn't ready to reinvest in furniture.

The other room downstairs would be my office. Its window looked out on the sheep paddock, a paddock that I was surprised to find also corralled a braying donkey. There was just enough room for my bodywork table behind the desk, although I wouldn't attract clients out there, out of town, and in a house so full of my own emotional debris splashed like an invisible but palpable Jackson Pollock all over the walls.

* * * *

I centered my solitary self-work up in the living room. Whether with crystal morning light streaming in, or later in the sharp silvery dusk, I invited music to fill the fresh, expectant space. My sound system and library of CDs dominated my day-life. I cranked the music up to motivate movement, as well as to drown out the sobs and wails and chuckles and screams. I let music bathe the wounds in my heart and soothe my starved skin as I writhed on the floor or wrestled with my fraught attractions to longing, arousal, and melancholy. I let emotionally stirring melodies feed my soul.

I delighted myself by making dances and songs out of all the accidents of movement and sound I stumbled on, turning chaos into pleasing forms through repetition and variations.

Sensing my weight grounded me in gravity, reminded me of both the sacredness and the ordinariness of my human body. Tuning my attention to the details of my inner experience, to the pleasures of slowing way down, to movement engaged at a glacial pace, and to the oceanic depths of motion and emotion reminded me that I was still anchored to my evolutionary origins and to the liquid body architecture I'd inherited.

I had no guru, no mentor, no therapist, no personal guide through that winter. I did the unwinding work on my own. But not without ample and reliable resources. My study with the pioneers in the fields of bodywork, mindfulness, somatics, and tantric and psychic spirituality had each left clearly marked trails for me to follow. Although I never felt devoted to the teachers themselves, their work, their methods, their attitudes, and approaches guided me. And I referenced all of it through my own body.

In my daily meditations, my sitting posture swirled and oozed within minutes of beginning a conscious controlled breath. Keeping only a deep, slow pattern of inhale and exhale, I gave over to the primordial flow that got underneath the holding in my body. Recognizing this inner movement as an authentic need, I participated with it. I gave amplitude to the waves, and rode them out to the far edges of my fingers; then let go and let them suck me back into my gut.

That movement back into center reminded me to power-pump the life charge coiled in my pelvis and to focus on the subtle sensual undulations of my pelvic floor. I ignored the whispers of socially induced shame that threatened to squelch the pleasure in my body. If that led down an erotic path, I followed it willingly. I encouraged it, even, by adding in a tantalizing brush of my fingertips on my lips, then a sensual stroking of the side of my neck with the back of my hand. And if I'd stoked the wood stove downstairs with sufficient logs from the shed outside, and if there was a patch of sun heating the carpet, I shed all my clothes to offer more skin to be caressed by fingers of warm air.

* * * *

And each day I took to the woods. The natural canopy sheltered my exposed nerves. The soft earth sponged away my yearning. The throngs of trees and undergrowth camouflaged my wandering and masked the sound of my out-loud and unrelenting arguments with the dwindling echoes of Michael's voice in my mind. Through the snow that occasionally blew in off the Blue Ridge that winter, or in the striped slivers of sunlight that slipped sideways between the trees, I trudged along the horse trails for miles, meeting no one.

Some days I felt great and told myself I was ready to move on. Other days I grieved heavily and loudly—grieving not for the loss of the relationship, but for the loss of my dreams. How was I ever going to realize the transformation through erotic spirituality that I longed for—that I had been hoping we would eventually get to, Michael and I? Without a steady partner to rely on, and to practice intensely with, how could I ever trust another man enough to let go into bliss?

Part of me was desperate to have a chance encounter in those woods, with the hope it would turn into a spirited friendship or passionate tryst—the part of me that didn't want to do the hard work of self-examination and heart scouring—the part of me that wanted to ride away in another relationship, to sail smoothly over the churning sea beneath—the part of me that was still resisting the idea that the soul-building treasures I sought could only be found by diving deep into my unconscious.

I acknowledged these parts but didn't let them distract me for long. Day after day, more exposure, more arousal, more breathing, more movement . . . all blended with the sounds howling out of my hollows. Doubt and ugly despair rounded up into cackles of crazy laughter. Rising crests of juicy pleasure slid down into troughs of gurgling desire. Long hours rode steady currents of thought after swirling thought. Heaviness of body gained mass, then gave way to suspended, weightless drifting. Longer roller-coaster whirlpools sank into delirious dream weaving.

Surfacing again, shaking off that murky underwater world of emotions, I would find my footing again, and feel my weight back onto solid ground. I'd stride into the everyday tasks of cooking and cleaning, reinvesting in an easy, lighthearted swing and sway. A trip into town for shopping and a yoga class would anchor me back into conventional social interaction.

* * * *

Days in that cabin in the woods were wild, and rich, and full of marvelous and welcome emptiness. Day after day overflowed with both the easy and the challenging. Nights, however, were just hard.

It was at night, after a well-deserved and carefully prepared dinner, that my emotional need for companionship slammed into me. Doubts and desires and delusions wormed their way into my brain. I paced around that little cabin, looking for something to connect to, someone. I talked to myself. I argued with myself. I imagined my fantasies coming true. And worse, I imagined none of them even drawing breath.

Nighttimes were harsh and detached from comforting sense-based reality. I lost countless hours in front of my computer, my gateway to the hall of mirrors that is Internet dating. I worked and reworked my own profile, trying on new definitions of who I intended to be, how I wanted to be seen. I studied profile after profile of the men there, trying to read between the lines, trying to imagine the gem of a man beneath the sad and sorry exteriors and expressionless descriptions they presented. My hope and my honesty eroded through the cautious back and forth that led nowhere—the endless fishing, hooking a nibble, reeling him in, only to find no one at the other end of the line. I got so disgusted with the amount of time I was wasting sitting in front of that little screen with no resulting skin time, I would punch off the computer and vow not to open it again. But the next night, or the one after that, I would be back.

As the winter lost its hold on the land, and spring gave rise to even more sexual energy and desire for connection, I finally realized I needed help. I needed someone to help me sort my way back into contact with the world, someone to confirm how crazy I was and possibly offer a lifeline back to sanity.

* * * *

The wise woman I engaged for a course of short-term therapy listened to me rant and rave and unravel my inner life for half a dozen sessions, quietly asking questions about this or that to better understand the razor's edge I had been dancing on. And then just as quietly, she pronounced me unambiguously sane and healthy. She helped me see that there was nothing wrong with the storms of doubt, heaving grief, raging desire, and now, this new surging of passion for sharing my life and my work.

She helped me recognize that I could trust my ability to swim deeply in the transformative waters of breath and movement and sound and emotion and then bob my head above the surface to gulp fresh perspective and chart the next tack in my flailing course. That I could howl and wallow in the darkest of emotional change and still witness and articulate what was going on—this was a gift. I'd built a fresh and sensual sense of self as well as new inner strength by being my own guide through the chewing, churning, and digesting of a life lost and a new life emerging. But now my hermetic life no longer served me.

So when a friend of mine needed a roommate for the house she was moving into, I jumped at the chance. Just the presence of another person each evening, with warm conversation and a good-night hug, transformed nights from hellish to earthly.

Later that year, a particularly violent storm ravaged the North Carolina coast, hitting head-on the part of the Outer Banks where I had retreated to clear my mind. From my new, shared living room, I listened and watched more closely as newscasters detailed the damage to houses, boats, cars, roads, and shoreline. With both horror and sadness, I realized that the half of a house they showed, ripped apart but still standing amidst its twisted framing and washed-out foundation, was the very cottage I had huddled in. The tatters of a white bead-board wall was all that was left of the bedroom I had curled up in to watch the sea-wind lash at the windows.

With quiet relief, I realized that the self-doubt that had thrashed at my thinking then merely littered the edges of my mind now. Although still halfway torn apart, and with more emotional debris still to clear away, I stood ready for the next phase of my life journey. I could rebuild on newly exposed foundations. I could rely on the body of evidence that had withstood the full force of my own emotional hurricane.

Isaac's Cigar

Carol G. Cutler

(Third place nonfiction, *Skyline* Summer contest, 2016)

The old Buick chugs up the steep, narrow road and winds around mountain after Buchanan County mountain as I ride with my grandfather, Isaac, on this warm summer day. Two cars meeting are inches apart, there is no painted line to divide the traffic, and passing is out of the question unless the car in front pulls over to the side at a wide spot—there are only a few of those, no shoulders, no guardrails. I can't look. These roads are typical for this county, named for the fifteenth president of the United States, James Buchanan, and in 1950 the poorest county in the state of Virginia.

It is rich in its natural resources of timber and coal, while the county government and many of its people are poor. Coal and mineral rights had already been sold by families who have lived on the land for generations, their potential value often grossly underrepresented to the unsuspecting landowners by outside developers who were buying the land first for timber, then coal and mineral rights. My grandfather, known to me as Pop Paw, and his brothers and father bought up some of this land, too, when he had a timbering business. His father, Elihu, the county treasurer for ten years, had already acquired a thousand acres.

The old-growth forests that once stood here were stripped from the mountains by the 1930s, floated out on rivers, and, later, carried by the Norfolk and Southern Railroad, which had built a spur line, to Knox Creek and along the Levisa and Dismal Rivers. Timbering is constantly in progress. Buchanan County is still the most forested county in the state.

I swallow fast to keep from throwing up. At eight years old, I hate to ask Pop Paw to stop because I am car sick, nauseated by the swaying side to side as the car rounds the curves. At least the windows are down and there's a little breeze. We go through a shady spot—thick underbrush, tall trees of many types on either side of the road. Now the big branches of the poplars, oaks, and hickories high up in the trees block the sun. Cooling shade covers the car, and I breathe in the fresh, cool, moist air. My nausea subsides. The Beechnut chewing gum my mother gave me to have at times like this helps, too. We left my grandparents' house in Honaker, Virginia, an hour ago, just Pop Paw and me, going to the Methodist church picnic in Davenport.

Never one to speed, as if we could on these curving roads and steep drop-offs, Pop Paw drives comfortably and happily, his fat stomach almost touching the lower part of the steering wheel. He has on a three-piece wool suit, with starched white shirt, tie, and diamond tie pin, even though the August day will be hot. But he'll take off the jacket later at the picnic and leave it on the car seat. The long-sleeved, starched white shirt and tie will be much cooler, even though he will still have on a thin tank top undershirt. I can smell the potato salad Granny made without my stomach churning too much. Thank goodness, the windows are down—not just for the nice breeze but also to let the stinking cigar smoke out.

"Now look on either side of the road here, Carol. Your great granddad Elihu bought 100 acres here in the '20s just before the Depression."

He takes the cigar out of his mouth to talk, holding it between his thumb and forefinger around a dry part of the tobacco just above a dark, soggy end that points toward his hand. This turns my stomach again for the worst.

"We took some timber out of here to sell at the lumberyard and Island Creek is interested in leasing fifty acres for coal mining." He keeps his eye on the road.

I nod and look out the window. He doesn't use a cigar holder like the picture he has of Franklin Roosevelt back at his house. Roosevelt clamps the stem between his teeth, looking up from the car he is riding in, a top hat, a big smile. Pop Paw has chew marks on the wet end that he puts back in his mouth and takes another puff. I wonder if he inhales that strong smoke. He takes his eyes off the curvy, narrow road to look at me.

"Are you OK?" he asks.

"I'll be OK when we get there, Pop Paw." I smile at

him. "I'm listening."

Maybe it's important to him that I listen, that someone listens, when he tells me about things like this—the land he takes care of, where it is, and what it looks like.

"I get a little car sick, so I'm not talking much," I add.

"Let me know if we need to stop."

He is familiar with my carsick problem. But I don't remember much about what he said; I remember the nausea I had on those roads. Now I remember, as my brothers probably do, too, how many times my parents stopped along the twenty-five-mile winding road from Cedar Bluff to Honaker that we drove in the 1940s, and '50s, each Sunday for dinner at Isaac and Gertrude's house. One day I would outgrow this queasiness I had in the backseat of my parents' blue Plymouth. Back then, sitting between Jim and Tom, my two brothers, on curving southwest Virginia roads, I would leap over one of them to throw up along the side of the road as they opened the car door as soon my father stopped the car.

"Let Carol sit by the window, boys," my father would say. No, they never came to cherish their baby sister, as I was called way past the time that I was.

That Sunday, Pop Paw and I are headed to a Boyd family reunion--that means fifty people, at least. It was just Pop Paw and me that day. My parents, aunts, and uncles were busy. My cousins were probably invited, too, but had other things to do. Granny often comes to these get-togethers. I think politicking is a primary objective for today and he knows I don't mind. I just like to be with him. He is nice to people, except a little too pushy when it comes to greeting people sometimes. We finally arrive as the tables are being set up on the lawn under huge oak trees.

"This is Carol, Alice's daughter," he tells one of the church ladies.

"She's staying with Gertie and me this week. Gertie's busy at home today, so Carol and I just drove over to see folks and catch up on what's going on."

"Why, howdy, Mr. Boyd. Nice to see you. Carol, put that potato salad down over here. We're getting everything set up."

The church ladies are very friendly and bring good food for the crowd. Lemonade and tea are in tall coolers with paper cups nearby. There are long tables, with pies, fried chicken, ham, deviled eggs, cornbread, and rolls spread out on white tablecloths, folding chairs all around, cars and trucks parked askew in the Davenport Methodist Church parking lot. Some of the ladies wear blouses, and little girls have dresses made out of the flower print sacks that once held the flour bought at the mill. My blue shorts and top are homemade, too. The women seem to float around the tables, straightening this or that, making room for more.

A loud car engine grinds and strains as someone is driving up the hill to the churchyard. There is not much flat land around here. Here comes another family from the parking lot, two little boys running ahead to join some of their friends already here. Men congregate in bunches under shade trees, smoking cigarettes, drinking what I guess is lemonade or tea.

I don't know anyone here---this is a different Buchanan County Boyd branch from the Isaac one--but Pop Paw knows nearly everyone and they know him. If he doesn't know someone, he goes up and asks another person he knows to introduce him.

"Rachel, I don't believe I know your friend." He looks at an older woman in a shirtwaist blue dress and straw hat standing with Rachel and three other people. She shyly smiles at the attention.

"Why, this is my cousin, Sally, Mr. Boyd." Rachel says, "staying with us to help tend the tobacco. We're way behind."

"Hello, Sally." He then grabs her and pulls her close and makes a big deal of kissing her on the cheek.

"Where you from?" he asks too loudly.

"Not far. Just up Contrary Creek." Sally seems a little uneasy, as he is right up in her face, but she grins back at my grandfather. Then she looks down at me and smiles. I like her.

"Now, who was your daddy?" Pop Paw always asks that when he meets someone new. Sally's husband stands with Rachel's husband, watching from over by the shade tree, as Pop Paw and Sally talk about her family. Rachel's husband, Richard, is smiling and elbows Sally's husband in the side. He knows that's Pop Paw. Everyone know how he acts. Pop Paw looks over there and waves for Sally's husband and Richard to come on over.

"How're you doing, Richard?" he asks, and Richard nods his head.

"What's your name?" he asks Sally's husband. When he says William, Pop Paw asks, "Now who was your daddy?"

After William tells him, Pop Paw tells a story about someone from the Contrary area. He bought a hound dog from a man who later went to prison for stealing livestock. His family asked if Pop Paw could use his influence in Richmond to get him out, which he did. When the man came back home, he came to see Pop Paw to thank him and asked for his hound dog back.

"I wouldn't steal from you, Mr. Boyd, so I'm asking you up front." It doesn't seem funny to me at all. I think the man learned a lesson by having to go to prison.

He pokes William in his stomach with an index finger and laughs louder than anyone. People shake their heads, smiling, and stand back. He looks at me out of the corner of his eye and sometimes winks at me when he tells a big joke. Usually, it's funnier to him than me. I am just glad not to be feeling carsick any more.

Pop Paw knows what happened around here for a hundred years back, at least. Even if it is a Boyd family reunion, everyone who goes to the church is invited. A lot of people now are milling around, laughing, and talking, holding drinks in paper cups, waiting for the lunch call and the blessing to be said. Where's the minister?

Cosette

(Third place nonfiction, Blue Ridge Writers Chapter contest, VWC, 2016)

My husband, Fred, and I first began naming the Canada geese on our Albemarle County pond in 1994. We didn't name them all—just the ones who distinguished themselves. Tony Soprano was a fierce fighter. Slo was always the last to scramble up the grassy bank on the far side of the pond.

The first geese to mate on our pond were Mabel and Max—no-nonsense names for no-nonsense geese. Max was constantly on the lookout for trouble, and Mabel built her nest near dense woods that protected her eggs. Eventually, when six goslings hatched, Mabel and Max exhibited the perfect combination of patience, discipline, and love that parents need.

It's remarkable for six goose eggs to survive the foxes, raccoons, and other hungry creatures that visit the pond, but six hatched goslings surviving into adulthood is quite a coup. Soon there would be six more geese flying and on their way to beating all odds. Mabel and Max were in complete control. That was until one scorching June morning.

"Something's wrong!" said Fred as we awoke to some desperate honking. Fred peered out the bedroom window that faced the pond. "Gerry, one of the babies is lying on its back, and the others are gathered all around it."

We hurried to the pond. As soon as we neared the young goose, the others moved away and stopped honking. She was waving her legs in the air and struggling to turn over, so I gently gathered her in my hands and set her upright. She hustled away from me to the water's edge and started to swim.

I breathed a sigh of relief. "There doesn't seem to be anything wrong with her."

Fred squinted in the morning sun. "Look how her leg's sticking out as she swims. She's not getting anywhere. There must be something wrong with her leg."

I threw some breadcrumbs in the water, and the little

goose, swimming in an unusual circular motion, made her way to the bread and ate it. "You go on to work," I said to Fred, "and I'll call the Wildlife Center."

Running up the hill, I waved good-bye to Fred and hurried inside. Soon I was speaking with an attendant at the center. She said I should bring the gosling to Waynesboro. Kruger Pond is located to the east of the Blue Ridge Mountains near Charlottesville in Central Virginia. The Wildlife Center in Waynesboro is on the other side of the mountains. I was sure I couldn't handle catching the goose and driving to Waynesboro by myself.

Dorothy and Bill, I thought. They lived across the street and had expressed an interest in the geese. I'll see if one of them will ride with me and hold her.

In no time Dorothy and Bill were at the pond, and I had prepared breadcrumbs for coaxing the little goose to come to me. She was used to me, but since she didn't know them, she refused to get out of the water and take the bread I offered.

"We could use the boat to catch her," Bill suggested.

"Good idea." I nodded back at him.

We decided too many people around the little goose was unsettling, so Dorothy left us and waited near my car. By now the sun was blazing, and Bill and I were both soaked with perspiration as we pulled the old fishing boat into the water. It hadn't been used for some time, and its green plastic seats were cracked, but it didn't leak. Soon Bill was rowing us toward the wounded goose. She was slowing down, but whenever we neared her, she got a burst of energy and took off.

"Look! She's hiding in the shadows of that tree." I pointed at a stately maple beside the pond. I picked up the towel that I planned to wrap around the goose, but she swam away from us again.

"Let's try one more time." Bill wiped the sweat from his face and set out again toward the exhausted goose. This time she had stopped to rest at the edge of the pond. Bill paddled closer to her than ever before, and I reached down into the water, scooped her up, and wrapped the towel around her.

"It's okay now. You're going to be all right," I

murmured as I cradled her in my arms.

"Everything's going to be all right," I repeated as Bill rowed us to shore.

We joined Dorothy, who was waiting in my car. After putting up a bit of a fight, our little passenger stopped nipping at poor Dorothy. I turned on the radio, and she stopped squirming and listened.

When our weary trio finally arrived, Dr. Kelly was waiting at the door. "So this is the Canada goose. Bring her right this way, and I'll put her in a crate."

The idea of putting her in a crate bothered me. But I was sure she was with people who knew more than I. "May I call and ask about her?" I was already uneasy about leaving her when I was the only human she seemed to trust.

"You may want to wait a day or two. We'll let you know when you can come to pick her up."

As Dorothy and I rode back home, I wondered how the rest of the geese would react to me after witnessing me snatch a member of their family and take her away. The geese at Kruger Pond don't trust human beings as a rule, immediately moving away to the safety of the pond whenever a stranger arrives. But I feel special every time they hear the sound of my voice, suddenly cock their heads, stand perfectly still, and listen. I talk to them every time I feed them, and they know I will treat them with kindness. I treasure their trust and the special bond we share.

When I returned from the Wildlife Center and went to their usual feeding spot with a cup of corn, they hurried to me as though nothing had happened.

"Listen, Guys," I told them as I threw out the corn. Some kept eating, but Mabel and Max cocked their heads and stood erect. "She's in the hospital. The doctors will help her leg get well. Then she can come back with you and learn to fly. You have to watch out for her because she won't be as strong as you. Don't let Tony chase her away from her food and never leave her alone. Will you do that?"

Mabel and Max stared at me and went back to eating. They hadn't run away from me, nor had they hissed at me disapprovingly. So far, so good.

That evening when Fred came home, he couldn't wait to hear what happened. "I thought about her all day," he said. "I even thought of a name for her. I'd like to name her Cosette after the little girl in *Les Miserables*. She had a miserable life until someone came to her rescue."

"That's perfect!" I said and gave him a big hug. "Hopefully her life will turn out as well as the other Cosette's."

For two days I waited to hear from the Wildlife Center and told myself no news was good news. The suspense of not knowing how Cosette was getting along was agonizing. I decided to check on her.

"She died." Those were the only words I remember. They hit so hard that I could barely stand. I felt numb and thought of breaking this terrible news to Fred.

When I met him at the door, he immediately asked, "What's wrong?"

"I called the Wildlife Center. Cosette didn't make it."

"She died?" I nodded and began to cry. "How did she die?"

"They didn't say." I fell into Fred's arms.

"I feel like it's my fault. I should have stayed with her longer. At least until she had something to eat. I should have held her and fed her, but I thought about getting Dorothy back home. She may have lost the strength to recover because she refused to eat."

Fred tightened his arms around me. "It was probably better that she die as she did rather than suffer a violent death from a wild animal."

I knew Fred was right, but I still felt guilty that I had left her when she must have been terribly frightened among strangers and probably wouldn't take food from them. I also knew that I would never again abandon an animal who trusted me as Cosette did.

As I recall the names Fred and I gave the geese in years past, I think back on how each was special is some way. I'll always remember Charlie's broken wing hanging down to the ground before he chewed off its feathers. I'll not forget the steady gaze of Mabel and Max or the beating of Cosette's heart as I held her in that towel next to my own.

Mother Nature's Fourth of July

BAMorris

(Honorable mention nonfiction, *Skyline* Summer contest, 2016)

The day was sweltering hot when my husband and I drove to my mother's house for the Fourth of July. That night my mother, Nick, and I drove to Kents Store for their fireworks display. A local man always donated the money to buy the fireworks, and the local fire department and rescue squad members set them off.

Dusk was just settling when we arrived. Dozens of families were spread out around the parking lot on blankets and the backs of trucks at the ARC Building. Children ran and played in the adjoining field, waiting for the show to start. The atmosphere was festive. We spread our blanket and then settled down to await full darkness. The fireworks were going to be set off in the field on the other side of the road from the ARC Building. A hush fell over the group as the first rocket flew up and exploded.

Almost at the same time, to our right, lightning flickered in the distance. We turned our heads from the man-made explosions to the natural fireworks. At first our concern was that the storm would head our way and catch us exposed. But as the storm intensified, we became more interested in the light show Mother Nature was putting on. We could hear the rolling rumble of thunder as it echoed across the sky. The lightning, which had started as single strikes, changed to bolts that branched out like downward tree branches. A single bolt would hit and instantly fan out to filled the sky. We were spellbound, watching the lightning instead of the colored lights put off by the fire department.

As the human show ended, the natural show in the sky moved down the river and out of our sight. We agreed that Mother Nature's light show far surpassed the one we had originally come to see.

Minus Two

BAMorris

(Third place nonfiction, Words on the Wall, Sixty-Eighth
Annual Philadelphia Writers' Conference contest, 2016)

I killed two doves today. I was on the way to the post office,
driving faster than I should have been. I saw what I thought
was debris, leaves or trash, lying in the road. I was going to
straddle it. The doves were huddled together, and when they
realized I was a threat and moved apart to fly away, I was on
them. I saw what they really were too late to slow down or
swerve to avoid them. I heard the thud under the car, and
when I looked in the rearview mirror there was a cloud of
feathers behind me. "Oh my god!" I whispered, but I kept
driving on my very important errand.

On the way back I searched for the feathers. I prayed I
wouldn't see the doves—that they had somehow escaped my
car. Then I saw one tiny body lying in the road. I pulled over to
the shoulder and put on my hazard blinkers. I picked up the
small body. It's feathers were so soft and the body was still
warm. The head hung loosely to the side until I cradled it with
my other hand. At first I simply moved the body to the side of
the road. The thought of cars squashing it into pulp made me
sick. Then I came back and searched for a more fitting place to
lay the body—something more reverent than a ditch. There
was a barbed wire fence on top of the bank with a cedar tree
growing beside it. I laid the little body gently in the roots of
that cedar. Then I went looking for the other body, half hoping
I wouldn't find it. But I did. It was on the opposite bank,
where my speeding car had propelled it. I picked it up and
carried it to lie beside its mate. I had blood on my hands from
each bird, both literally and figuratively, and by now I was
crying.

"I'm so sorry," I said through my tears. "Please, God,
forgive me for taking the life of two of your creatures. Forgive
me for this."

"I didn't mean to hurt you," I said to the doves.

I still grieve for my act. Humans are careless and unconscious. We think we own this planet. I am human, much to my sorrow.

My Stream-of-Consciousness Opinion, Relayed in Cliché

Lauvonda Lynn M. Young

(Third place nonfiction, Appalachian Authors Guild, VWC, 2016)

Donald Trump, the business mogul, wants to "make America great again." The "Donald" thinks he is well qualified to be the next president of the United States, seemingly because he is rich and has business acumen. Trump's money does nothing to enhance his eligibility to take possession of the highest political position in our country. The fact that Trump is ridiculously rich in spite of his many bankruptcies does not mean he possesses the intelligence, discipline, control of self, or experience to be the leader of our nation. Trump is the last person we should elect president of the United States.

Let me call a spade a spade. Donald Trump is incorrect in his assumption that he will make America great again. The United States long has been the greatest nation in the world, and in spite of all our problems and issues, it still is the greatest. There certainly are many problem, and laws "on the books" that should be reviewed and revised. Immediate attention needs to be given to our nation's infrastructure. Our tax system requires a total overhaul. The Affordable Care Act needs to be reviewed, mistakes corrected, additions made, or sections deleted so that the ACA will work more efficiently, ensuring success, so that the ACA will continue to benefit the individuals who have insurance for the first time, or those who can't afford other private health insurance premiums. We don't need to abandon the ACA. For once, let's fix it instead of starting over and dealing with a myriad of new or similar problems. We also need to take steps to ensure Social Security and Medicare will be available into the future, because, unlike the rich, many can't survive without these benefits. Medicare needs a review, as well, and, if necessary, a revamping.

Since we are in the season of electing a new president, I point out the dire need to overhaul our political process. Our primary and election process is outdated and overly lengthy. The timeframe needs shortening. Less money should be involved in the process—money that could be put to better use in our nation, and perhaps relieve some of the taxpayer's burden. There must be oodles of potential candidates who have the desire and potential to lead our nation. Yet, these bodies are not stepping forward, and we have to settle for less than desired. I'm sure many Americans have a mental list of needed change that would greatly improve life in the United States. My suggestion is that we, the people, use our voices, henceforth, to help bring about revision and modification. Voices joining in unison would have an impact. Grumbling within the walls where we exist, but taking no action, will not birth change. Battling in the streets won't produce transformation. Our joined voices and our votes can force change.

If Trump is elected, he will not be our savior. The "Donald" is in this race because he loves basking in the limelight and the presidency would put him on the world stage. Changing his residence to 1600 Pennsylvania Avenue for four years or more would solidify Trump's place in history books. It's a certainty the "Donald" would love all of the attention and adoration. One does not have to be cerebral to know Trump does not possess the experience, knowledge, or business acumen to quality him to be our president. Our nation does not need a famous television celebrity who entertained us in the past by producing the Miss USA Pageant and a reality show.

To say it differently, I don't want a leader who carves his life into a reality show, nor do I wish for the Oval Office to be the location for the reality show. The "Donald" has a short fuse, and he goes on the attack when someone tells him something he doesn't want to hear. On national television, Trump made reference to a woman's menstrual cycle; he suggested one of the Republican candidates in the primary, a woman, had an ugly face, by asking, "Who would vote for that face?" Trump made references on national television about his private parts, which was crude and unprofessional.

Many say that Trump loves to battle. While our president will have many different battles to deal with during his term, we don't need a person who wants to skirmish about stupid things. We want a person who can deal effectively with a national or world crisis that requires military intervention or another problem of great magnitude. I shudder when thinking about the "Donald" leading our nation. A president needs to know how to negotiate, to be calm under pressure, to be able to work with discordant personalities. First and foremost, our president has to be a leader, a leader the world can embrace, support, and rely upon.

I have no doubt Trump would continue to be divisive if he were elected president. He already has cocooned himself in discord. Trump may be able to bully his way with his business associates, those who work or deal with him, and others, but he will be forced to trek a different path if he becomes our president. We, the people, do not have time to give Trump on-the-job training. For all of the aforementioned, and more, I state emphatically, the "Donald" would be a disaster as president of our nation. Wait, I need to say more.

One of the worst messes to roll out of Trump's mouth was the statements he made on national television about abortion. Mister Trump, Mr. Know-It-All, believes a woman who has an abortion should be punished. He espouses a man requires no chastisement. Really! Since a man is 50 percent responsible for a pregnancy occurring, I believe the male needs to assume half of the responsibility when a woman is impregnated. Unfortunately, the "Donald" seems really to believe what he said about abortion, although, after a backlash, he retracted his horrendous statements, by saying he would not make changes in the current abortion laws. Mister Trump can paddle backward all he wishes, but it's too late for him to put the toothpaste back in the tube. A zillion apologies won't help now. My view of Mr. Trump plummeted even lower after he blotched the issue about abortion. He showed his stupidity. People should take note. While my following statement deviates from the issue at hand—that is, Trump and his candidacy—if I could have a face-to-face with Trump, I would tell the "Donald" he and all men should get out of the business of telling women what they should do with their bodies.

Another one of Trump's bloopers was his declaration that Mexicans are rapists. He followed those words, or preceded them, by adding when he is elected president, he will build a wall to keep illegal immigrants (especially Mexicans) from entering the United States. I haven't encountered anyone who thinks a wall is feasible or that a wall would be effective. There certainly needs to be a review of our immigration laws and related issues, but building walls already has proved ineffective, so another solution is needed. We Americans should show a little compassion; many immigrants helped establish our nation; numerous foreigners are currently performing jobs in the United States that our white-faced section will not fill, and, no doubt, many of them have Green Cards. No doubt many are nationalized citizens. Yes, there are illegal immigrants, but there are many ways for illegals to get into our country other than climbing, or trying to climb, a wall. While Trump's statement about building a wall was bad enough, his assuming, "All Mexicans are rapists," is way over the top.

Another outlandish statement by the "Donald" is his saying he will end the country's national debt within a short number of years after he becomes president. Good luck with that—I'm not going to hold my breath. It would be wonderful for the United States to be debt free, but even if there was a possibility of success, it isn't going to happen in four-to-eight years, unless our government seizes everyone's wealth. Most of the sentences that spurt out of Trump's mouth prove him to be as dense as a London fog. We don't need a buffoon in the White House. Mister Trump's faults and gaffs are numerous. I wonder how well the "Donald" would function, if say, Vladimir Putin, came calling to forge a new deal with President Trump. Enough said. If Trump is our next president, the entire world will start laughing.

Please, let's closely scrutinize Trump, the candidate. Sending Trump to the White House would open Pandora's Box. Okay, I know no one is perfect. Hillary Clinton has her negatives, but, hey, Clinton has the most political experience.

She not only has held important governmental positions, such as senator and secretary of state, but Clinton also got up close and personal with politics as the wife of a president and governor—her spouse, who valued her opinions and insight. Bernie Sanders would be acceptable, but Sanders does not have Clinton's political savvy and her experience with foreign dignitaries. Don't judge me wrongly. I like Sanders. Maybe Clinton will make him her vice president. The other Republican candidates are going to wilt soon, so they are noncontenders at this point in time. Bottom line: Hillary has the experience, knowledge, and willpower to lead our nation effectively.

I hope I haven't stirred up a hornet's nest by stomping on the "Donald," especially by those who plan to vote for him. Just keep in mind that we can't make a silk purse out of a sow's ear. Trump is too ensconced in himself to change significantly at this stage of his life. The best advice I have for Trump supporters is for everyone to give careful thought before checking Trump's name on the ballot, because that genie can't be stuffed back into the bottle at the end of election day. Trump inhabiting the White House and becoming our national leader is akin to a skunk showing up at a lawn party. Let's avoid attending that event.

Adventures in an Italian Garden

Linda Levokove

In the long blades of grass I see a pair of almond-shaped blue eyes. I come closer and an adorable gray kitten scampers down a dirt depression. I come closer still and peer down the hole. The gray kitten is snuggled up against his tiger-striped sibling and I wish I could cuddle up with them.

I wander around the garden, debating as to which spot could be my bed for the night. The concrete bench is not my first choice. Maybe I could curl up against the shed with the tattered tan blanket that's lying on the ground. I could tuck my legs under a pile of dry leaves.

I gaze up at the faded umber and apricot stone walls of the monastery. Some pigeons coo on the tile roof. They stand on either side of the roofline and look like bookends. Other birds fly by tweeting sweet arias, and on the ground a profusion of wild roses thrive along the old brick wall to the right. The stone-floored courtyard is pockmarked with depressions of century-old footprints.

Walking back up the stairway to the door that had locked behind me I realize there is no other way out of this garden. I hear a window slam below and loud voices arguing in Italian. Maybe just a lively conversation. Both sounded the same to me. A cacophony of pots bang around. Pots and voices. That's good.

I walk down a short flight of steps and the voices get louder. "Hello." I shout. "*Bonjourno*." Being embarrassed is better than sleeping on the ground. "Hello. *Bonjourno, Bonjourno*." Finally, a lull in the chattering and a burst of Italian from the nuns who are cooking dinner in the basement kitchen below ground.

"*Aspasti*," comes the reply. I wait. A door opens and one of the sisters, in full habit, walks up the few steps. "*Degurie mia*," she says, motioning me to follow her. I walk behind her down more steps into a long dimly lit hallway, past the kitchen, and then up another flight of steps, when I realize I'm in the front reception room where our group had checked in only an hour before. I sigh in relief.

"*Grazi, grazi milleone.*"

"*Prego,*" the nun says with a wink and a grin.

ON WRITING AND PUBLISHING

Tell Better Stories

Lori Dixon

I talked recently with an acquaintance who had just judged a large short story contest in another part of the country. She offered me an interesting perspective on her judging experience. All the stories she had read were technically competent—even skillful, all written by people who studied their craft and obviously could write. What surprised her was that most of the stories themselves were, as she put it, "mediocre." Not the writing, but the stories, the plots. The writers had put all their energy where their teachers and role models told them to—on the craft, and they did it so well they forgot the first rule of writing: tell a good story. In the end, the factor that gave one entry a First Place and another an Honorable Mention was that intangible: a good story, one that draws you in and nestles itself into a small place in your heart.

As writers, we spend a lot of time working on technique. It's essential. But that focus makes us often forget that technique only equals competence with our tools. Woodworking makes for a good analogy: in order to carve wood, you have to master the chisels and knives; you have to know your different woods and their hardness, their densities; you have to practice; you approach a piece of raw matter with the right pressure in your hands and angles in your mind. That's all technique. But *what* you carve is art. To be an artist requires a partnership: technical mastery and vision. We spend a lot of time on technique, but not nearly enough on vision. A life's worth of technical ability will make you a mediocre writer if you can't wed it to a compelling vision.

You must remember to tell a better story. The art of the tale is as important as the skill of the teller.

This holds true for poets, as well. And I think for poets it's harder. For one thing, we have fewer role models. No one can teach what poetry *is*, let alone how to master it. You can teach technique. Technique is a requirement, yes—the love of language for its own sake, the study of prosody, the mastery of form. But then, once the forms are mastered, what then?

Poetry as an art cannot be taught; it must be *learned*. Beginning poets almost always fall into one of two groups: overly personal or overly public. Neither is a place to linger.

William Wordsworth wrote that poetry is "the spontaneous overflow of powerful feelings: it takes its origin from emotion recollected in tranquility." Since then too many poets have believed that inspiration and personal vision are all you need. Generations studying poetry as an academic literary form have developed for us an image of the Poet Archetypal. A poet is exquisitely sensitive, attuned to deeper rhythms of life, the kind of person lampooned in an old *New Yorker* cartoon of a bucolic meadow, a group of laughing people sitting on a blanket and chatting over sandwiches and wine and an angst-ridden, isolated fellow off to the side looking distantly past the margin. The single panel is titled "The Poet at the Picnic." Poets are supposed to be filled with introspection, sensitive souls battered by the world, Chatterton in his attic, Keats done in by a bad review.

Yes, *of course* you need personal vision. After all, the poem is an intensely personal form. But you need more than personal vision, and this is where too many beginning poets are badly guided. A poem should not be so personal that it's impenetrable. A reader can't get inside; a great many poems are just that. This kind of poem opens the poet's heart, but remains closed to the reader's.

Because of copyright issues and my desire not to make enemies I can't use any contemporary poet as an example, so, with apologies, I'm putting forth one of my own early failures. At the time I wrote it, I was playing with form and syllable count, seeing if math equations provide enough poetic structure to establish form.

Fission

Five o'clock
winterborne dark, wrapped
in a quilt to catch the sun
rise I wait.

Stars blaze and fall
phenomenon
I've been told. I wait
shivering. Inside
a chilly room, a tossed
bed, one half asleep.

Another phenomenon. Above
in patient mindless progress
a satellite falls
dying west.

Yes, the poem is intensely personal. Too personal. As it happened, an acquaintance who edited a small literary magazine asked me to contribute a poem, and I gave him this one. He was not satisfied. Instead of asking for changes, he published the poem as follows:

Fission

Five o'clock
winterbourne dark, wrapped
                    to catch
the rise I wait,

Stars blaze and fall
phenomenon
I've been told,
Shiver. Inside,
a chilly room, a tossed
bed, one half asleep.

Another phenomenon. Above
in patient mindless progress
a satellite falls
dying west.

This is the rare occasion when an editor changed a poem to make it *less* comprehensible.

Aside: I think every poet has had this happen at least once—your work is changed without your permission. This editor never asked me about the edits; he did them on his own. And even though the poem is not particularly good, it was mine. I felt the violation intensely. This was a case of editorial malpractice: an editor should *never* change your work without your permission. Never.

Still, the experience was not a waste, as I took two lessons from it: 1) editors are not infallible, and 2) the fault was as much mine as his. The poem was too personal, the symbolism too private. I didn't let him inside; he could not find his way in and did not understand it. That intense personalization allowed him destroy the structure and make a hash of my poem.

That lesson could not have been taught—it had to be learned. The story was good, but the imagery too closely held to make the poem successful.

Too personal is one extreme. More than half of the entries in the poetry contests I've judged are personal to the point of impenetrability. Now, you may think, "yes, but aren't there poets who created their own symbolic systems, resonant with meaning?" Yes: Yeats and his gyres, Eliot and bricolage, Hughes and Crow, Oliver and the woods. These are symbolic *systems* that poets developed—and this is key—over the course of a career, deepening and feeding the imagery as they went along. And you can still read any one of their poems without relation to the system, and enjoy the poem. Seeing the repetition of language and image across a collection or a career deepens its resonance, but the image is accessible on its own. None of their poems are impenetrable.

The obverse impulse is also a problem: the Public Poet Persona—the poet at the lectern, declaiming Truth to the Masses. The poet at the lectern is the poet who hides the self behind a public mask It's a strategy that speaks *at* readers, not *to* readers. Even if the poem is clever, it's superficial.

The examples that come first to mind are public poems. You know them—they're often titled something like, "Polemic: _____." Public poems can celebrate specific occasions, like inaugurations. In that they're like odes, which also commemorate discrete events (except odes are usually awesome). Public poems, however, react to a public event; they don't meditate on it. They're almost never good, unless they're written by Maya Angelou. Fair use in copyright allows me to quote only a few lines as illustration. This comes from the poem that Robert Frost meant to read at John F. Kennedy's Presidential inauguration, titled "Dedication":

> Come fresh from an election like the last,
> The greatest vote a people ever cast,
> So close yet sure to be abided by,
> It is no miracle our mood is high.
> Courage is in the air in bracing whiffs
> Better than all the stalemate an's and ifs. (lines 54-59)

I want to be clear that picking out a few lines (not even the most groan-worthy lines) from a single fifty-five year old poem is unfair, especially a poem that is meant to celebrate a public event in an official way. These poems are flourishes that ornament special days and aren't meant to speak deeply to the individual. What surprises me is how many poets adopt the same strategy for their own work. I've served as a contest judge for a number of years, and it surprises me that usually a fair sprinkling of entries fall into the Public Poet spectrum. The poet hides behind the poem. The poem is a work of the head and, lacking an emotional component, it feels superficial and preachy.

These two extremes are common in amateur poetry (remember that *amateur*, from the Latin, means *a lover of*). Poets who publish widely find a way to synthesize the two poles. As a poet, you should aim to strike a balance between the personal and the universal. Tell a good story. Even if your poem is short, a reader should be able to glean a history worthy of a novel in its few lines. If you want examples, look at the contest winners in this volume. The poets balance head and heart; they examine experiences that are intensely personal, yet universal enough to work in the reader, as well.

The art of poetry cannot be taught; it must be *learned*. You teach yourself, and the path you take will be the one of your own forging. You'll get a feel for it. This is art at its most mysterious. It's catching quicksilver. It's like juggling while walking backward on a balance beam. Work on the technical skills to make it look easy and natural, and teach yourself the art. As long as you know what you're working toward, as long as you keep the image of the ideal poem in your head, you'll get there. You'll learn to trust yourself. Tell better stories. You'll know it when you find that balance. Your lines will sing

Let Me Tell You

Erin Newton Wells

The moment heads straight for me. I know it well. The question is polite, no offense intended. It ought to be an easy reply. It is not. If the true answer were desired, the question would not be asked this way.

She mentions an interesting thing to do, a place to go. "I can't," I say. "I have work I need to finish." By now I could learn to keep the gate shut, but I continue to swing it open. I always hope for an eager response to step through and greet me.

"What work do you do?" she asks. Here's the dilemma. Do I tell the job that earns money or the one I really mean? I am honest. Since I allowed the gate to open, I now accept the consequence of what stalls before it. "I am a writer," I say, and wait for it.

There is confusion over the word as spoken. "Really?" she greets it with enthusiasm. "Where do you ride?" It is clear that equestrian sport is a great conversation starter. Her face is bright. I will soon change that expression.

"I am a writer," I repeat, enunciating clearly. Her expression falls. "Oh," she says. Then, trying to relate this to something she understands, she assumes I mean novels on the *New York Times* bestseller list. First comes, "Well, tell me something you've written." Then, "Where can I get it?"

I have nothing to offer her in the fabulous avenues where she wishes to walk. What I must tell her next always brings pure silence. "I write poetry," I say. Yet even here, after a space of no words and the totally blank look I know so well, she tries once again to bring me into the fold of something useful she can handle.

"Oh, I love poetry. Tell me something you've written and where I can get it." Or, "I remember a poem I read in school." Or, "Show me one of your poems." I should pull one out of my pocket like a coin? Recite one on the spot, perhaps my grocery list spoken majestically? I decline. I feel I owe the

199

children of my brain the proper time and setting for their first steps into her world.

Poetry in our present society often is regarded as a lace doily with satin ribbon. It is the cute pet of literature. Or it is named the tofu of the arts, shunned as weird, a substitute for the real thing, such as a thrilling novel. Why is it so difficult to have a discussion of it with someone other than another poet?

Much effort has been made by poets and poetry foundations to promote what has fallen on hard times in the public sphere and become a poor stepsister. Poets laureate often develop projects to build understanding that dispels a fear or distaste of poetry. They demonstrate that it is not silly or useless and that there is no reason we should lose face with our peers by reading or writing it. Writing poetry well is one of the most difficult things to do and one of the most rewarding, not in the monetary sense, of course.

The poet selects and works with only a few words. Dozens are discarded before the right ones come together in exactly the right phrases so the right sounds and images are evoked in mind, ear, and eye of reader and listener. The words suggest a truth without directly saying so. To bring forth this lean thing is strenuous and exhausting work, underpaid and misunderstood. It is also exhilarating. I would not wish to do anything other.

Writers often compare their work to breathing. When asked, "Why do you write?" meaning why put up with this no or low pay and little recognition, many respond, "Because I must." I've often thought I should move to Wales where poetry festivals harkening back to ancient times are still held and bards are honored. Or perhaps that, too, has changed. Poets in early societies were the ones who sang history and current events, preserving and telling what needed to be known and remembered.

Poetry once was not thought merely a thing of pretty ribbons. It was news, enthralling drama and documentary, heartbeat of top current songs. It still is. Read the respected contemporary poets. They are a mirror and voice of our times. Their words strongly and directly engage in the world right now in which we live. They compare the present world to its past and to possible things to come. Poets see the world's largeness in something which may at first seem quite small and insignificant, and they must tell it in so few words.

At its best and as it is intended to do, poetry says something of importance to its receiver but without smacking him directly on the head with it. The poem invites him to find his way to it through an open gate. How do I tell this to the person who asks what I do, who politely tries to show interest, and who clearly does not know how to take the first steps?

I could refer to the words of Auden, that no poem is completely true but that a good one will make us desire the truth. I could quote so many other poets and offer thoughts of my own. Writing poetry is hard and useful work. To the person who asks what I do, listen and let me really tell you. Give me time and I will try to show you. It is about you and worthy of your attention.

Using Improv to Improve Your Writing

Deborah M. Prum

A couple of years ago a friend coerced me into taking an improv class. She pestered me for months, both in person and via sending texts, e-mails, and links to class registration. I finally relented.

So, our first class I found myself in a small room with a ragtag group of people (a fireman, physician, teacher, neurosciences researcher, playwright, chauffeur, pastor's wife). What were our instructions? Among other things, in that session we learned to say "yes" to one another, to listen to each other, to join each other in flights of fancy, to maintain a consistent portrayal of the character we created (voice, tone, point of view) and to think tangentially.

I had no idea what I was getting into. I didn't know how profoundly my training in improv would affect my life. Soon after taking classes, I approached painting, playing music, and public speaking differently. Moreover, I used elements of improv to help me improve my writing.

Both writing and performing improv forces me to engage in two different types of cognitive activities. Both writers and performers need to stay within a specifically proscribed form. People tend to think that improv is a completely off-the-cuff performance. It's not. There are certain rules performers must follow when interacting on stage. Even the show as a whole has a specific structure. So, improv performers follow particular conventions in order to create scenes, just as writers follow grammar/syntax/vocabulary/spelling rules while creating their work. Both performer and writers must pay attention to the rules in order to communicate clearly, yet at the same time, they also must be innovative. That is, both groups need to think creatively in nonlinear, unpredictable ways. Both groups work to combine incongruent concepts or images to produce a new, unique entity.

Applying improv techniques to my writing process has helped me be a better writer. Saying "yes" is one of the first concepts you're taught in improv. For me, with regard to

202

writing, saying yes means believing there exists a creative flow within me and I need to go with that energy, not sabotage it. How does one cooperate with creative flow? Get rest. Write in a comfortable environment. Let your brain relax and receive ideas. Don't show your work to people who will squash your little beating heart. Do show your work to people who can provide honest, intelligent feedback. Be resilient in the face of rejection. Try not to be fraught with anxiety when you arrive at a pausing place in your writing, realizing that you will have more to say and the ideas will come. For example, I've just finished the thirteenth chapter of a new novel. I'd say I'm close to midway. It's a screwball mystery of sorts. I have a good idea of how I'll end the book, but I'm a little foggy on the next step. What will chapter fourteen look like?

Ideas have not yet flooded into my mind. So, I'm taking a break. I'm letting the field lay fallow for a bit. I took a dance class this morning. I edited someone's essay this afternoon. I'm going to garden later. I believe the ideas for chapter fourteen will arrive soon. I'm being positive and saying "yes" to my rhythm of writing and resting. I'm saying "yes" to my belief that there is a creative flow within me and it will keep flowing.

Another invaluable aspect of improv is developing the habit of listening. Many of my writing ideas are inspired by merely attending to the people around me—not only what they are saying, but also what they are not saying, how they use and misuse words, their idiosyncratic phrases (like "might could" and "you best be quiet now" or "she had a frisky bladder"). I love hearing people tell stories about their relatives, people like Daddy Two Fingers and Aunt Baby. After I get permission from the storytellers, on occasion, some of these folks show up in my writing.

Since taking improv, I'm far more diligent about consistency and believability when I create my characters. I think about motivation, what makes my character tick. In the new novel I'm writing, there is a character named Little Jimmy. All he cares about is finding an enormous amount of money that he believes is hidden close by. He ignores his daughter, doesn't even glance up when a pretty woman passes by, is willing to steal a car and shoplift. He'll do anything to find the cash.

So, when I write Little Jimmy into any scene, I keep his motivation in the forefront of my mind. My mantra is, "What would Little Jimmy, the money grubber, do?" I make sure every action he takes and every word he speaks coincides with his motivation to find that money.

Last but not least, using improv techniques helps me when I am trying to address plot issues and figure out story flow. As improv performers, we are trained to think beyond our first responses to a question, not only beyond first responses, but also out as far as we can imagine going. This way of thinking helps to generate nonderivative, fresh ideas. Dead ends turn into wide-open roads.

So, I have two words to say to that pesky friend who harassed me into taking improv. Thank you!

Advice to New Novelists

Jack Trammell

Sometimes other writers come to me and ask for advice, and I am always happy to share. Although I am not a *New York Times* bestseller (yet), I have had a few small successes, and so here for your perusal are a few thoughts.

To get an agent or not get an agent?

Usually, if you ask this question, you're already answered it—it means you haven't had an agent before, and you probably would do better being represented by one. I had an agent helping me with my first novel (*The Saints Departed*—please, please don't look that one up . . .) and frankly I wouldn't have gotten it published without his help. With that said, I have published other novels without an agent, so it is possible to do so. But in this day and age, for a novel to receive critical acclaim or sell very well an agent is almost always part of the equation—they are the gatekeepers to the largest publishers. There are still university presses, smaller publishers, and self-publishing options, including print on demand (POD), but the novels we *ALL* know about are almost exclusively published with the help of an agent.

How do you get an agent? There are standard formats to make queries, although you will likely find that many agents don't accept new clients or are difficult to communicate with. There are also tiers of agents just like there are tiers of publishers, and you should set your sights only on agents who represent the kinds of books that are like yours and are accepting new clients. In many ways, securing an agreement with an agent is tantamount to securing a publishing contract, as legitimate agents will not take on books they don't think they can sell.

If you don't want to self-publish or tinker with more literary presses, start practicing cover letters AND think about how your social network might connect you with someone in the business. Don't be afraid to network shamelessly in seeking the right agent.

What about self-publishing?

Self-publishing doesn't carry the stigma that it used to, but it still has one big problem—usually you don't sell any books after friends and family are done purchasing.

Print on demand is a nice option that keeps your book in print forever, but with more than one million new books every year, being in print *forever* isn't as long a period of time as it used to be . . .

What about eBooks?

When eBooks first came out, it was the next big publishing frontier. Now, eBooks are a niche, but limited market. It turns out that people still like holding paper-bound texts in their hands and licking their fingers to turn real pages. (Sorry, that's gross and unsanitary.)

Now eBooks are not generally exclusive publications but rather another version of a mainly print book. I wouldn't try to make the first big splash with an eBook that isn't also a print book—it didn't work that well even for the great Stephan King, so your chances are limited . . .

So back to small presses and university presses

Small presses and university presses are making a comeback. Like craft beer, small-batch whiskeys, and organic food, they do have a special place in the publishing world that eBooks and crony capitalism couldn't totally kill. In fact, I predict they will flourish more in the next ten years.

If you choose not to get an agent (or for whatever reason you are not successful in getting one) but you remain convinced that you have written a great novel, you may want to try a publisher who is regional, niche, or independent and works with nonagented authors. Some of these publishers do charge some fees for certain parts of your contract (even though they are NOT vanity presses). They usually don't offer advances on royalties, either. Never-the-less, they publish hundreds of darn good books every year that often to get some critical acclaim, and sometimes sales that go beyond your Facebook friends.

In conclusion

There are more options open to authors/novelists than ever before. You can even publish your own books with POD services, and for many people this is "good enough."

But if you're serious about cracking the door with a bigger publisher, and the feedback you are getting to this point from colleagues and others is encouraging, then pursuing a literary agent is probably a solid idea.

By the way, there are a ton of agents out there. Do your homework first and find out who does what, who their clients are, and what they are looking for. In my experience, letters work much better than e-mails; also remember to just wear out your social network finding out who knows who. If your novel is that good, when someone sees it they will recognize that—finding them AND getting them to see it is the key.

Good luck! Let me know when I can get my signed copy.

The Dictionary Is Your Writing Partner

Gary D. Kessler

A story is meant to be a partnership of shared understanding and appreciation between the author and reader, not an author's "just try to understand what I've written" game (well, for most of us). The dictionary is an aid to writers (and readers) in making this happen, and there is a way to "read" the dictionary to take much of the burden of "what is right and what is wrong" off the shoulders of writers to a greater extent than most authors seem to realize. Here are a few tips for "reading" and using the dictionary in U.S. publishing style to take some of the guesswork out of spelling, hyphenation, and capitalization decisions and to free the author's time for the creative aspects of writing.

First, there are basically two types of English-language dictionaries. There are **descriptive** dictionaries that focus on telling you the latest information available on "what is" in word usage. *Merriam-Webster's Collegiate* dictionary is one of these kind. And then there are **prescriptive** dictionaries, such as the *American Heritage* dictionary that focus on telling you the "why" of word usage. Both kinds of dictionaries are trying to help writers make the best and least obtrusive choices in word usage. And many writers miss the boat named "Opportunity" by not using the dictionary enough or fully enough—and most editors would have been able to see through a veil of sloppy writing to see content issues better and to improve an author's story significantly if the author had used the dictionary more. Although it's good to consult both types of dictionaries when working with a word meaning, this essay will concentrate on the descriptive dictionary, and, in particular, *Merriam-Webster's Collegiate* dictionary (which isn't just in print; it's available for free use on line as well).

U.S. publishing has selected two descriptive dictionaries as its spelling/hyphenation/capitalization authorities. These are the best to use simply because the whole point of such standardization is to make the presentation of a story as transparent and understandable for the reader as possible so that the reader can concentrate on the content of the story itself.

The standard style guide for U.S. market fiction and nonscientific nonfiction publishing is the *Chicago Manual of Style* (CMS—because nearly all publishers accept this authority so that there will be a recognized standard). The CMS, again for the sake of making life simple and understandable and word renderings transparent for the reader, has identified two dictionaries as "best choices" (CMS, 2.51). The absolute best is *Webster's Third New International Dictionary*. Almost no one, including publishing houses, actually uses this, though, because it is so humongous in bulk that it requires its own special table to reside on and you'd need a crane to move it across the room. To use it, you'll have to get up from your desk and go to it; you also will have had to lay out big bucks just to own it. This leaves the latest edition (currently the eleventh) of the *Merriam-Webster's Collegiate* dictionary as the one of choice.

The smart writer won't fight using this dictionary—the author will just be relieved the publishing industry is helping by reducing the number of wheels that have to be reinvented each time you sit down to write a story.

(A couple of asides on the *Webster's* dictionary. First, "Webster's" is a generic name identifying a style of dictionary, not a company name. And, although the current edition of *Webster's Collegiate* dictionary is the eleventh edition, this dictionary is actually updated every time there is a new printing, which is a couple of times a year. And this is why the publishing industry has chosen it for its descriptive dictionary. It updates current word usage every couple of months. Of course, this also means that that "latest" edition you bought yesterday will, like all those damnable Microsoft products, no longer be the "latest" information a couple of months after you'd laid out twenty-five bucks for a copy. But you can access it on line for free.)

OK, then, how can learning how to "read" dictionary entries help the writer? If you learn just a few pointers on what the dictionary is trying to do for you, you will save time and worry about whether you are making the best spelling, hyphenation, capitalization choices. This will both keep you from waking up in a sweat in the night wondering why you spelled *that* word *that* way and make more time and energy available to you for the creative aspects of story writing.

Spelling

Webster's Collegiate dictionary has built-in pointers on how best to spell a word:

Any word entered is spelled correctly in normal writing. U.S. publishing, however, wants words spelled in as standard a way as possible so that readers don't trip over them or stop to consider whether they agree with a spelling chosen, and thus lose the flow of the story. So, in the U.S. publishing style, the first-listed choice is the standard. For instance, in normal writing the renderings "judgment" and "judgement" are both proper spellings (as long as you stick to just one version throughout the work), but the dictionary helps you identify which one the U.S. publishing industry prefers. If you go to that word, you will find the listing "judgment or judgement." This is signaling that the first-listed form ("judgment") is preferred. (The "judgement" rendering is British style.)

And speaking of "signaling," if you go to "signal" to see the declension of "signaling," you'll see "signaling or signalling." This is telling you that, although "signalling" is acceptable in normal writing, the first-mentioned version, "signaling," is the preferred spelling for story writers in the U.S. publishing world.

So, look for and use the first listed rendering. That's the preferred choice. Zero sweat for you if you just go with the flow. It's the story elements that are the creative writing process, not the word spelling.

For the U.S. style writer, the dictionary will also identify British variation spellings (which are just fine in the British system, but shouldn't be found in U.S.-style stories). Under "labor," for instance, you will find the full listing definitions. And under the British equivalent, "labour," listing, you will find "*chiefly Brit var of* LABOR," which is telling you that "labor" is the best choice (in U.S. style writing). It probably won't even include any definition at the "labour" listing. This is a "duh" signal that this isn't where the action on that word is if you are writing in the U.S. system.

If you find the term *trademark* behind an entry (e.g., "Dolby"), by law you have to spell and capitalize it exactly that way. You can use it in your writing, you just have to spell it as trademarked (and, no, you don't need to put the registration mark, ®, behind it).

Hyphenation

Probably the most head-scratching puzzle in the realm of spelling decisions is what to hyphenate. The dictionary will help with some of this (but not all of it—there are all sorts of instances like combined adjectives, for example, "blue-eyed girl," and special cases like "six-year-old-boy" that aren't spelling issues. Similarly, combinations can be treated differently depending on where they are in the sentence, for example, "She was given the heart-to-heart talk" but "The talk she was given was heart to heart." These sometimes would take a masters in grammar to work out correctly, unfortunately, so we'll just ignore them here. This is about simpler, more understandable basic good habits you can develop).

The dictionary shows much in the way of proper hyphenation, and the basic *Chicago Manual of Style* rule is that if you find the term in the dictionary, follow its lead on hyphenation, and if you don't find the combined-word term in the dictionary, don't either hyphenate it or run it together— leave a space between the elements (CMS, 7.85). The general rule of CMS on hyphenation is, "if in doubt, don't." (And don't be Germanic and run all of the elements together in one long glop, unless the dictionary tells you to.)

One of the stickiest issues with hyphenation is use of hyphens for prefixes, like ante, anti, bi, bio, co, counter, extra, infra, inter, intra, macro, meta, micro, mid, mini, multi, neo, non, over, post, pre, pro proto, pseudo, re, semi, sub, super, trans, ultra, un, and (*whew*) under. Authors seem to love to set these prefixes off with hyphens, and in nearly every case they were wrong to do so. The dictionary can help you make decisions on when a hyphen for such a prefix is in order (almost never). If you find it hyphenated in the dictionary, than hyphenate it. And if you don't, don't—run the elements together without a space. If you look at the dictionary right where any of these prefixes would be listed alphabetically, you'll find a long list of words showing that they aren't hyphenated. Chances are good the word you are looking for is on that list. The dictionary people took the time to run those long lists to try to help you shake the usually wrong-headed hyphenation habit, and U.S. publishing has been antihyphenation (see what I did there?) for a good long time, something that computer spell check doesn't seem to understand. Computer spellcheck is nearly hopeless on hyphenation.

Capitalization

Being able to read a dictionary can also help in capitalization decisions. (And, like hyphenation, the rule of thumb is "when in doubt, don't." No, English isn't so close to German that we capitalize every noun.)

If the word is always capitalized, it will be listed that way—for example, "Friday" (and not "spring").

If an element of a term is capitalized but other elements aren't, it will be listed that way—for example, "Parkinson's disease."

If some forms of the word are capitalized but others aren't, it will be listed in lower case and identify when it's capitalized—for example, "**swede**: *cap*, a native or inhabitant of Sweden; (not cap), a type of rutabaga."

Abbreviations (using full caps) will be listed in full caps—for example, "AIDS."

Formal titles preceded by prefixes (with, in such cases, do take hyphens) will be shown as they should be rendered—for example, "Neo-Expressionism"; "off-off-Broadway."

Dialogue in Fiction

You are not bound by dictionary spellings in dialogue rendering where you are trying to show voice patterns, regional dialect, or education levels of characters, for example, "sheeet" for (you figure it out) or "gawd" for "God" or "pul-eeze" for "please." What you should do, however, is to remain consistent for that character.

Bottom Line

The *POINT* is that, just by learning a few tricks of being able to read guides to "best choice" word decisions in the dictionary—and by actually turning to the dictionary when there's the least bit of question that you are rendering a word or word combination correctly—you, as an author, can improve the presentation of your stories significantly, free up time and energy for the creative aspects of your writing, and improve your connection to and appreciation by the reader.

These have been just few, basic pointers on reading the dictionary. If you want to become a master at it, charts and discussions on what the information given in a dictionary entry means—and can help you—can be found in the first thirty-two pages of *Webster's Collegiate*. Taking time to read these sections will be a real eye-opener to you on how the dictionary can save you effort and confusion and become a full writing partner that gives you extra confidence in your writing and provides extra clarity and trust in your readers.

ABOUT THE AUTHORS

David Black ("Poor Man's Rain" and "Live Birds, Dead Birds," poetry), a retired English teacher and minister, is a former poetry editor of the *English Journal* and a frequent contributor of poems, essays, articles, and reviews to small magazines and academic journals, especially in the Appalachian region. He is the author of two books, *Some Task, Long Forgotten and Other Poems* and *The Clown in the Tent*.

Carol G. Cutler ("Isaac's Cigar," nonfiction), who enjoys writing nonfiction, fiction, and poetry, lives in Albemarle County in the foothills of the Blue Ridge. She has published research as a clinical specialist and teacher of psychiatric nursing. She's active as a hiker and amateur naturalist and being with the families of her three children when they are available. She appreciates being in writers' groups in the Charlottesville area.

Lori Dixon (*Skyline* Summer contest poetry judge; "Tell Better Stories," writing/publishing) wears numerous hats: medievalist, teacher, house restorer, novelist, poet, farmer, long-term cancer patient, decipherer of obscure handwritings. She gets bored easily and tends to juggle too many projects at once. She lives in a great old house, talks to herself, and practices hack and slash gardening. As the sun goes down, she can most often be found by a fire, next to the river, in good company and with a couple of dogs. She has been honored to judge contests for the Virginia Writer's Club and the Poetry Society of Virginia.

Phyllis A. Duncan ("Reset," fiction; "Verses for Orlando," poetry) is a retired bureaucrat but one with an overactive imagination—at least that's what everyone has told her since she first started making up stories in elementary school, prompted by her weekly list of spelling words. A commercial pilot and former FAA safety official, she lives and writes in the beautiful Shenandoah Valley of Virginia. A graduate of Madison College (now James Madison University), she has degrees in history and political science. Her love of politics continues to this day. Her fiction has appeared in numerous literary journals and anthologies. When not writing, reading, reviewing books, singing, watching the Yankees, or cheering on Dale Earnhardt, Jr., she takes delight in spoiling her grandchildren.

Stan A. Galloway ("To Know the Heart," "Canadian Prairie Gothic," "Pond Dance," poetry) teaches at Bridgewater College in Virginia's Shenandoah Valley. His poetry includes *Just Married* and three chapbooks. His reviews of poetry have been published in such places as *New Orleans Review, Callaloo,* and *Paterson Literary Review*. His book of literary criticism is *The Teenage Tarzan*. He is founder and host of the Bridgewater International Poetry Festival.

Jody Hobbs Hesler ("Baby-Faced Wolf," fiction) lives and writes in the foothills of the Blue Ridge Mountains. Her fiction, feature articles, essays, and book reviews appear or are forthcoming in *Gargoyle, The Georgia Review, Streetlight Magazine, Sequestrum, South85, [PANK], Steel Toe Review, Valparaiso Fiction Review, Prime Number, Pearl, Potato Eyes Journal, A Short Ride: Remembering Barry Hannah, Charlottesville Family Magazine,* and other places. One of her stories was a Pushcart Prize nominee and several have won regional contests, including the Virginia Writers Club Golden Nib and UVa's Writer's Eye, and appear in prize anthologies. Currently earning her MFA in Fiction from Lesley University, she has also enjoyed fellowships at the Virginia Center for the Creative Arts and has conducted writing workshops in area schools for students from third through twelfth grade.

Lois M. Holden ("Hidden Truth," fiction) lives in Nelson County, Virginia. She started writing poems as a child and has continued to write poetry and short stories since those early efforts. She has worked as a publisher, technical writer, book editor, and newsletter editor. Her entry, "Old Sukie and Me," won first prize in the 2013 Fralin Museum of Art (University of Virginia) Writer's Eye competition in the university/adult prose category, and her short story, "An Ordinary Day," received an honorable mention in the 2014 Writers' Eye competition. The short story "The Hearing Aide" won honorable mention in the Blue Ridge Writers Chapter 2014 writing contest. In 2015 her short story, "Target Practice," won third place in the Blue Ridge Writers contest. She is a member of the Lonesome Mountain Pros(e) Writers Workshop, the Blue Ridge Writers Chapter of the Virginia Writers Club, and the Virginia Writers Club.

Sarah Collins Honenberger's (*Skyline* Summer contest fiction judge; "Robert Frost Where Are You," fiction) novel, *Catcher, Caught*, is a Pen/Faulkner Foundation selection in its Writers in Schools program. Audio, German, and Korean editions have been released. With numerous short fiction awards and a fellowship from the Virginia Creative Arts Center, she appears regularly on literary panels and at book festivals. Her other novels include *Minding Henry Lewis* (2014), *Waltzing Cowboys* (2009), and *White Lies: A Tale of Babies, Vaccines and Deception* (2006).

Gary D. Kessler ("On the Cusp," fiction; "The Dictionary Is Your Writing Partner," writing/publishing) is a former news agency managing editor, diplomat, newspaper columnist, theater critic, movie consultant, book editor, and publishing consultant. His published works include the short story collections *On the Downtown Mall* and *Shadow of the Blue Ridge*; volume editor for the two-volume *WritersNet Anthology of Prose* and the four-volume *Blue Ridge Anthology*; coauthor of a publishing reference, *Finding Go! Matching Questions and Resources in Getting Published*; a mystery novel, *What the Spider Saw*; and, most recently, the memory book *Of Me I Muse*. He has won or placed in multiple Virginia Writers Club annual contests and the UVa Art Museum's Writer's Eye prose contest and took third place in the John Gresham–judged *The HooK* short story contest in 2011. His poetry has appeared in the *Piedmont Virginian*. He also writes pen name mystery novellas and novels.

Gerry Kruger ("Cosette," nonfiction), a native Virginian, moved in 1979 from Richmond to the Charlottesville area. She taught English for twenty-seven years at Charlottesville High

School. Since 2004 she has participated as a judge in the Writer's Eye Contest, sponsored by the University of Virginia's Fralin Museum of Art. As an essayist on National Public Radio, she detailed the adventures of a lame Canada goose that arrived at her pond on foot in 2000 and stayed with her for nine years. Her first book, *On Kruger Pond: Charlie's Story*, chronicles her unique relationship with this goose and his struggles and triumphs. Gerry hopes to publish another book, which will contain Charlie's story as well as more recent essays about Charlie's descendants that continue to visit the place where they were hatched. Ultimately she hopes to record all of the essays for the blind.

Joy Merritt Krystosek ("Grace Merritt," poetry) lives in Madison County, Virginia. Joy is the published author of two cookbooks, *Cooking Chicken with Joy* and *Cooking Savory Comfort Foods with Joy,* and a book for children of all ages, *How Many Stars Are There in the Universe?* She is in the process of publishing *The Life and Death of Jacques Albèrt Rainelle,* an interactive adult historical fiction and art book. Joy and three other writers in the Lonesome Mountain Prose Writers Group published a collection of their work in 2014 titled *We Grew Wings and Flew.* Joy is a member of the Blue Ridge Writers Chapter, the Virginia Writers Club, Lonesome Mountain Prose Writers Group, and the Poetry Society of Virginia.

Martha Jean Lancaster ("Celestial Immortality," fiction) is collections manager for The Fralin Museum of Art at the University of Virginia. She is currently the curator of an exhibition on collections care and art conservation that will be on view from March through August 2017 at the Fralin. Ms. Lancaster is a Richmond native and descendant of French Huguenots and English who settled Virginia in the early seventeenth century. Her publishing history includes short stories and essays in the *Blue Ridge Anthology*, the *Skyline* anthologies, and the *Richmond Times-Dispatch*, as well as awards from the Virginia Writers Club, Blue Ridge Writers Chapter, and the Writers Workshop of Ashville, North Carolina.

Susan M. Lanterman ("The Stranger," poetry; "Fearless Flying," "Trains, Planes, and Autobuses," nonfiction) writes human-interest stories for the "Commentary" section of Charlottesville's *The Daily Progress* newspaper, is writing a collection of short stories based on her Charlottesville B&B, and is concluding work on a young adult novel, "Hasta Luego, Santa Claus," which follows the antics of a teenager and his family of illegal immigrants.

Linda Levokove ("Petals in the Wind," poetry; "Adventures in an Italian Garden," nonfiction) is the author of two collections of poetry: *Walk on the Heart Side* and *Cabbages & Kings*. She is former vice president of the Blue Ridge Writers Chapter of the Virginia Writers Club and a member of the Poetry Society of Virginia and the Virginia Writers Club, which has presented her with a Special Award for Outstanding Service and Contribution to Poetry in Central Virginia. In addition, she has participated in the Virginia Festival of the Book, teaches a Poetry Critique Group at Olli/UVa, and has presented her poetry at several public venues. Presently Linda is working on a collection of poetry and short/short stories.

Sigrid Mirabella ("Stealing Sweet Briar," poetry), originally from Long Island, New York, defines herself as a social hermit and hopeful skeptic living in rural uncertainty. Her works have won awards and have appeared in *The Blue Ridge Anthology*, *Mid-America Poetry Review*, *Skyline, prose and poetry*, *Long Island Pet Gazette*, *Lynchburg News and Advance*, *Dog Fancy*, *Woman's Day*, *Countryside*, *People Magazines* and various Macmillan/Howell books. In her other life, she works for a humane society in Nelson County, Virginia.

BAMorris ("Mother Nature's Fourth of July," "Minus Two," nonfiction) is a retired teacher. She lives with her husband in Central Virginia. She began creating stories as a child. She writes short stories, memoirs, essays, and poetry.

Becky Mushko (*Skyline* Summer contest nonfiction judge; "One Owner," fiction), retired Roanoke City teacher and

2006–2007 writer-in-residence for Roanoke County Schools, currently serves as vice president of Lake Writers and is a lifetime member of the Virginia Writers Club. She has self-published (*Patches on the Same Quilt, Them That Go*), vanity-published (*Peevish Advice, More Peevish Advice, The Girl Who Raced Mules & Other Stories, Where There's A Will*), small press-published (*Ferradiddledumday, Stuck*), online-published (blog *Peevish Pen*), and e-published for Kindle (*Them That Go, Patches on the Same Quilt, Stuck, Over Coffee, Rest in Peace, The Best 'Un Yet, Miracle of the Concrete Jesus and Other Stories, Ferradiddledumday, and Little Meg Reddingoode*). Her stories have appeared in *A Cup of Comfort for Writers*, volumes II and III of the *Anthology of Appalachian Writers*, and many other publications. A three-time winner of the Sherwood Anderson Short Story Contest and five-time winner of the Lonesome Pine Short Story Contest, she is best known for her wins in the infamous Bulwer-Lytton Bad Fiction Contest—"Worst Western" (1998) and "Vile Pun" (2008). She blogs at http://peevishpen.blogspot.com; her Web site is http://www.beckymushko.com.

Gwendolyn Thompson Poole ("If God Gave Me Wings," fiction) enjoys creating fictional characters for stories and plays set to the backdrop of slavery and the Civil War, particularly in the Shenandoah Valley area of Virginia. One of her most rewarding writing achievements was her play, *The One Called Peter*, commissioned by the Oliver Community Center in Winchester, Kentucky. This dramatic piece was an adaptation of the life and times of former Kentucky slave, Peter Bruner. She recently won recognition from the Blue Ridge Chapter of the Virginia Writers Club for her story "If God Gave Me Wings." Gwendolyn was born in Lexington, Virginia, but currently resides in Greensboro, North Carolina.

Deborah M. Prum ("Over the Moon," fiction; "Using Improv to Improve Your Writing," writing/publishing) is the author of *Fatty in the Back Seat* (a young adult novel), *First Kiss and Other Cautionary Tales* (an audiobook collection of humorous essays that first aired on NPR-member stations), *Czars and Czarinas* (an anecdotal and interactive history in iBook format) and *Rats, Bulls and Flying Machines* (a print book about the Renaissance). Her award-winning short fiction has been published in many places, including *The Virginia Quarterly Review*, *The Blue Ridge Anthology*, and *The Sweetbay Review*. Her humorous essays appear in many places, including the *Washington Post* and Charlottesville's *Daily Progress*, and air on NPR-member stations. Her work can be seen at www.deborahprum.com.

Sara M. Robinson ("Click Bait," poetry), founder of the Lonesome Mountain Pros(e) Writers' Workshop and Instructor of a course on Contemporary American Poets at UVa-OLLI, is poetry columnist for *Southern Writers Magazine* and poetry editor for the premier issue of *Virginia Literary Journal*. In addition to publication in various anthologies, including *We Grew Wings and Flew* (2014) and *Scratching Against the Fabric* (2015), and journals: *Loch Raven Review*, *The Virginia Literary Journal*, and *Poetica*, she is poet and author of *Love Always, Hobby and Jessie* (2009), *Two Little Girls in a Wading Pool* (2012), *A Cruise in Rare Waters* (2013), and *Stones for Words* (2014). Her latest poetry book, *Sometimes the Little Town*, released in February 2016.

Elizabeth Doyle Solomon ("Waste Land," "Lesson from Oenothera," "The Oak Tree's Swing," "Summer's First Firefly," "Shenandoah Sunset," and "July Gifts," poetry; "My Oklahoma Summer," nonfiction), a New Orleans native and retired teacher, began writing at age eleven and publishing at age thirteen. Now in her seventies, she reckons her poems total over 60,000. Elizabeth has published two poetry collections, *Season*s and *The Steering Wheel Poems*, written newspaper columns, and founded the *Central Virginia Leader* newspaper. Her recent awards for both poetry and prose have come from the Poetry Society of Virginia, the Blue Ridge Writers, and the *Skyline* anthology. Until recently, Elizabeth led the Blue Ridge poets' critique group in her home, every Friday, for fourteen years. She is working on her third book, a collection of poems and short stories, *Journey West and Everywhere*.

Olivia Stowe (*Skyline* volume editor; "Tightrope Walker," fiction) lives and writes in Central Virginia. Stowe's specialty is cozy mystery novellas, which include a thus-far ten-volume series of Charlotte Diamond mysteries, the most recent of which was *Fowler's Folly*. The Christmas season short stories, "Cassandra's Last Spotlight," "Blessedly Cursed Christmas," and "Jesus Speaks Galician" add to this series. She also is the author of the inspirational Savannah novella series. Stowe's standalone mysteries include *Fiddler's Rest, Restoration of the Castle,* and *Final Flight.* Her inspirational Christmas short story collections are available in the *Spirit of Christmas* and *Christmas Seconds* anthologies. This is the fourth annual volume of *Skyline* she has volume edited in conjunction with Cyberworld Publishing.

William E. Sypher ("Let's Pretend," poetry; "The Execution: Riyadh, Saudi Arabia," nonfiction) worked as an English professor for twenty-six years in five Middle Eastern countries: Iran, Saudi Arabia, Bahrain, Qatar, and Oman. Living in the desert, under a mostly featureless sky, inspired him to populate that canvas with images, but he paints only with words. Thus, he resorted to writing essays and poems drawn from life there. While in Oman, he was asked to describe poetically what photographers do. He wrote: "Too much light and they might as well have photographed the sun itself. Too little, and they have captured only the darkness. Between these extremes photographers dwell; they are the keepers of the modest light." Writers are not so constrained.

Roger Tolle ("My Body as Evidence," nonfiction). After years as a professional modern dancer in New York City, Roger Tolle built a successful practice in Trager Movement Education. His writing about this work was published in *Massage Therapy Journal*, Melbourne's *NOW!* magazine, and in the videos and body reminder cards on his Web site, www.RogerTolle.net. He currently teaches professional trainings and personal growth workshops around the world and works as a Surrogate Partner for men going through sex, intimacy, and relationship therapy. He writes and travels from his base in Charlottesville, Virginia.

Jack Trammell ("Snake Bit," fiction; "Advice to New Novelists," writing/publishing) lives on a farm in Central Virginia, where he is a modern agrarian and a recognized voice of Appalachia (born in Berea, Kentucky). His writing credits are diverse, ranging from hundreds of poems, articles, and stories to larger book-length projects and academic research related to his college teaching. His most recent book, released in 2016, is the coauthored *The Fourth Branch of Government: We the People*. He is a trained historian, a research methodologist, and an environmental advocate, but most of all he is committed to the act and art of writing, as well as encouraging others in their personal literary journeys. He can be reached at jacktrammell@yahoo.com.

Leonard Tuchyner ("Untouchable Garden," poetry; "Still a Mountain to Go," nonfiction) is a semiretired counselor, living in Central Virginia with his wife and two dogs. He maintains an active involvement in the local writing community, which includes participation in a writing critique group and in the Blue Ridge Writers Chapter of the Virginia Writers Club. Although challenged by legal blindness, he continues to pursue Tai Chi and related forms of martial arts. Gardening is another passion that has captivated him for most of his seventy-six-year life. One of his most fulfilling endeavors is the facilitation of a Senior Center's Writing for Healing and Growth writing group. He has been in the winners' circle of the Blue Ridge Writer Club's yearly writing contest several times. His winning entries have included poetry, fiction, and nonfiction. He has also been a regular contributor to *The Blue Ridge Anthology*. Mr. Tuchyner has published essays, poetry, and short stories in *Dialogue Magazine* (for which he is now a columnist), *Magnets and Ladders*, *Nomad's Choir*, *Westward Quarterly*, and *Skyline*. A poetry book, *A Journey to Elsewhere*, was published in 2014.

J. Elizabeth Vincent ("Transgressions," fiction) began writing fiction at the age of fourteen with the help of her best friend and her ninth-grade English teacher. She wrote much then but did not publish. In her mid twenties, she served as a coeditor of a small literary magazine, *The Unknown Writer*. After the birth of her first child sixteen years ago, J. Elizabeth published many nonfiction articles and a book under her real name (Janell E. Robisch) before recently rededicating herself to fiction writing. She joined the Blue Ridge Writers Club in 2015 and is grateful for the comradery she has received as well as the chance to enter the contest that produced this story.

Erin Newton Wells ("Locus," and "A Fish," poetry; "Let Me Tell You," writing/publishing) has taught studio art for many years in a school she established in Charlottesville, Virginia. She has been writing all her life and is now becoming more active publicly, especially with poetry. Currently her writing appears or is forthcoming in *Poetry South*, *Spillway*, *The Sow's Ear Poetry Review*, *Poetry Virginia Review*, *The Poeteer*, *Form Quarterly*, *The Piedmont Virginian*, *The Writer's Eye*, and *Skyline*, among others.

Lauvonda Lynn M. Young ("I have my mother's lips, those she imparted upon her first of six" and "I Remember," poetry; "My Stream-of-Consciousness Opinion, Relayed in Cliché," nonfiction), author of the poetry collection *Just a Woman*, writes in various genres, including poetry, fiction, nonfiction, and memoir (mostly fact based). She has been published in anthologies, newspapers, magazines, and other sources. Lynn plans, organizes, moderates, and presents programs and workshops. She served as a member of the Executive Committee of the Poetry Society of Virginia for many years and was the program chair for the annual poetry contest and annual awards ceremony in 2014 and 2016. Lynn is serving in an advisory role in 2017. Past president of the Blue Ridge Writers Chapter, Virginia Writers Club, Lynn received the VWC Superior Service Award in 2011. She holds memberships in the Appalachian Authors Guild (VWC), Blue Ridge Writers (VWC), Poetry Virginia (PSV), Virginia Writers Club, and WriterHouse.

Skyline 2016

The third collection of works by
Central Virginia Writers.

Skyline 2016

Olivia Stowe, ed.

*Prose and Poetry
by Central Virginia Writers*

Skyline 2015

The second collection of works by
Central Virginia Writers.

Skyline 2015

Olivia Stowe, ed.

Prose and Poetry
by Central Virginia Writers

Skyline 2014

The first collection of works by
Central Virginia Writers.

Skyline 2014

Olivia Stowe, ed.

*Prose and Poetry
by Central Virginia Writers*

www.ingramcontent.com/pod-product-compliance
Lightning Source LLC
Chambersburg PA
CBHW072233170626
46813CB00003B/1199